ARCO AUTOMOBILE LIBRARY

1949 Cadillac, body by Saoutchik

Famous Old Cars

1936 Cord

by Hank Wieand Bowman

1930 Ruxton

1930 Packard

1931 Duesenberg

ARCO Publishing Company, Inc.

New York

CONTENTS

A 1938 Horch 853 Series special sports convertible coupe is shown above in three views. Courtesy A. J. Koveleski. Photos by Fred Honig.

Fourth Printing, 1978. Library of Congress Catalog Card Number 57-14442.
ISBN 0-668-00597-1 (Library Edition). ISBN 0-668-04311-3 (Paper Edition).
Printed in the United States of America.

FOREWORD

A famous old car, more commonly referred to as an automobile classic, is a car of "acknowledged excellence"—one that evokes vivid recollections of motoring at its best. Such a car could have been a Ford or a Wills St. Claire, a Rickenbacker or an Essex. Who's to tell a motor enthusiast what car spells classicdom? Literally thousands of different brand names have been on the market; each make has had its champions. Maybe for you a Seven Little Buffaloes, a Leach-Biltwell or Kurtz Automatic can whip up fonder memories than a Grabowsky, a Car-Nation or a Crane Simplex? Of this group, the latter would get my vote.

The names attached to cars have had little effect on their sale or their quality. The Ludinghaus-Espinshied was a tongue twisting flop but even today many people who mispell or misplace the origin of the Duesenberg speak reverently of the big D. Peerless was high blown sounding and its producer stayed in business for nearly thirty years while Paramount, Perfection, Acme, Triumph, Victor and Ultimate with equally grandiose names failed in short order. The Classic—and there was a car by that name—was strictly a dog. The Black Crow played an uninspired part on the automotive stage; the Black-Hawk by Stutz will long be remembered while the Red Wing, Eagle, Falcon and Sparrow winged rapidly into oblivion.

There was a King, Queen and a Princess but none were destined to become enthroned as automotive royalty and today the names Wasp or Phianna, Locomobile or Stearns-Knight are far more likely to warm the collector's heart. The Sun, the Moon and the Star have all been eclipsed. The Only and the Everybody's are no longer anybody's. The Pickard lasted four years; Packard is still an honored name.

Your own favorite car may not be listed here for thousands have rolled across the motoring set. But among the automobiles described and pictured are many of those generally credited with classic status due to mechanical superiority, exceptionally fine or lavish body work, advanced styling, outstanding performance or a combination of any or all of these characteristics.

In gathering materials for this book, I have received willing assistance from many other car enthusiasts. In particular I wish to express my thanks to Ted Kavenagh of the Classic Car Club of America. Others who have offered me considerable help include: A. J. Koveleski, Raymond DeVos, Ferris E. Alger, Wendell F. Chapelle, Capt. John Leydon, USN, Henry A. Clark, Jr. of the Long Island Automotive Museum, Edmund Robinson, Bill Callahan, Frederick Thorsen, J. O. Goodell, D. J. Wendling, Preston A. Reed, Thomas H. Hubbard of the H. H. Franklin Club and Peter Shavney. Many others have been helpful in permitting the use of photographs of their favorite cars in this book and to all who contributed I am grateful.

Hank Wieand Bowman

Introduction

Rolls-Royce's 1907 Silver Ghost is a true classic.

You don't have to be bound by the strict rules of the Classic Automobile fancier if you are an Automobile Classic enthusiast.

THE difference between the *classic automobile* and the *automobile classic,* or famous old car, may sound like so much double talk, but a definite distinction does exist. Today, as production line cars take on more and more of a similarity of appearance and mechanical design, a new type of automobile connoisseur has come into the foreground. These collectors have been pushed into their new hobby because of a desire to own and drive a piece of rolling stock that is individual in appearance, mechanical design and handling characteristics. In other words, the automobile classic enthusiast is a guy who doesn't want to own or drive just another pea in another pod.

The hot rodder would rather be caught dead than sit behind a piece of rolling stock with a single exhaust header, a power plant of stock compression ratio or unaltered body lines. To the rodder nothing is so sweet as a composite bomb built up from a '32 Z-ed frame, with a coupe body of different vintage, lowered in profile, powered by a late model full-bored, heated-up V-8.

The sports car enthusiast, by contrast, will sacrifice nearly anything for what he terms handling characteristics—the ability to corner a lightweight, unadorned car at fantastic speed over twisting, high-camber roads.

A different breed is the horseless buggy fancier who gets more bang out of digging up and restoring a 1901 One-Lunger with tiller steering than finding a new Cadillac convertible in his Christmas stocking.

There is also the far larger group of late model stock enthusiasts who believe sports cars, hot rods and antiques are strictly for squirrels. Although not organized in clubs, their mutual and greatest thrill is derived from weekend waxing of their late model Detroit product, boasting of the ease and intricacies of its push-button window controls, hydraulically operated seats and the pleasures of clutchless driving with power steering.

A fifth group consists of the classic car

Rarely seen today, the Marmon Sixteen with its 1930 LeBaron-built body, designed by Teague, was a real standout in appearance and performance.

A classic in advanced design, considered too radical in 1934, the Chrysler CU Airflow Eight had its power plant located directly over front axle.

Low slung, excitingly styled and sprightly for its era, the 1917 Chalmers Speedster has enduring beauty, foreshadowed today's sports car design.

In 1933 this dual-cowl Cadillac V-16 phaeton-bodied car develcped 165 horsepower at 3,400 rpm from its 452.8 cubic-inch displacement power plant.

collectors. The C.C.C.'s are as fanatically devoted to their cars as any of the other groups but about the only thing they have in common with those other clans is a love for power on four wheels. The classic car has been roughly described as an automobile manufactured between 1925 and 1942. That this very era selected by some classic car enthusiasts does not have universal appeal is evidenced by the antique fancier's scathing reference to this same period as the "Ugly Thirties."

The Classic Car Club of America feels that the true span of the classic period is not set by dates but by standards of style and performance—or during a period the classic car lover describes as the "Golden Age" of car design. This group considers that the Golden Age began sometime just prior to the Depression, its traditions enduring until the outbreak of World War II. Whatever its chronological limits, the era marked the high point in the evolution of the automobile, for the classic was produced at the peak period of real natural wealth, in a day when neither price nor priority was an effective barrier to the use of best materials. It was constructed and serviced by true mechanics, men who understood the total functioning of every engine component, a long haul from the assembly line robots who make and maintain the world's cars today.

The line between the antique automobile and the classic car is strongest in the field of performance. A classicist invariably admires, may even collect and restore antiques, but he does not feel that these lattice-trimmed, bicycle-built specimens ever included anything approaching a perfect car. The self-propelled buggy was a pioneer vehicle, splendid as an experiment but wretchedly designed and almost completely impractical.

Conversely, the classic enthusiast rejects the modern stock car as the optimum of nothing but bad taste, for he knows that in the development of the motor car, the clas-

The Packard Twelve (twin six) of 1934 had a 144" wheelbase, weighed 5,400 pounds. In custom-built sport phaeton form it was an outstanding product of its day and is much sought after by collectors.

An entire cult of Lincoln Continental worshipers has sprung up in recent years. Many claim that the 1940 sedan, above, was the forerunner of today's hard-top convertible. Undoubtedly a true classic in every sense of the word, the Mercedes-Benz 380 chassis, below, is a typical example of the fine workmanship that went into many old cars. Chassis is electrically welded, has independently sprung wheels.

sic represented a peak which has never been surpassed. He views the current models as bath tubs on roller skates, lineless balloons even less picturesque than the cough-wracked gigs and rattle-haunted coffins which became prehistoric with the dawn of the Golden Age.

Not wholly in contradiction with the classic car enthusiast is the automobile classic lover for whom this book has been written. This group will in time perhaps comprise the largest of all automobile fan memberships. Yet, they may well never have their own club organization nor is it probable that competitions will be arranged specifically for its members, since these are the limbo condemned car fanciers, the collectors and fans without representation by house organs, rule books or clubs.

The automobile classicist in distinction to any of the preceding groups is primarily a four-wheel romanticist. His enthusiasm for automotive products knows no restrictive bounds of specific years, design periods or country of origin. To him the automobile classic may be a product as exciting and contemporary as the Mercedes 300 SL or as mechanically fascinating and non-representative of its period because of its then advanced design as the fabulous Rolls-Royce Silver Ghost of 1907. The automobile classicists have only one thing in common with one another: they are connoisseurs of four-wheeled power plants; they appreciate and respect beauty of line, fine engineering, outstanding performance or a composite of all three. But unlike the other five groups, they are not automotive snobs. They don't view the Doble, the Stanley or the White as tea pots but rather are fascinated by and admire the smooth, effortless power of the Steamers. Too, they are not financial high hats. To them a well-built car in the under $3,000 class is frequently to be as much admired as the somewhat more refined car with a price tag of six grand and upward. They don't necessarily consider production automobiles of this decade as rolling caskets and have great respect for the present day product—when it offers a distinction that makes it a standout in luxury, dignity or engineering from other production cars.

The classic automobile fanciers are frequently beset, too, by contradiction in hidebound rules of their own making. They insist that the true classic must be custom bodied. This embarrasses them somewhat in accepting into the fold the magnificently engineered Marmon V-16 of 1931 which with its massive 145-inch wheelbase, boasted one of America's finest designed power plants but only a ho-hum body that was pleasing but not exciting for its day. That the body wasn't custom built has caused some of the classic car purists more than a few hours' loss of sleep. The classic automobile fancier nearly always insists that his cars must be big, expensive and luxuriously fitted out.

There *is* a definite distinction between the classic automobile fan and the automobile classic fan, with the latter cherishing most of the cars so dear to the heart of the former, but with no treasonous feeling in giving the antiques and some contemporary models an equal degree of admiration. The automobile classicist knows no boundary and has no set of ground rules which force him to reject a product because it was built a year too soon or two years too late, or because it didn't set its owner back a king's ransom. He is merely a lover of all fine and distinctive cars. It is the purpose of this book to picture and describe his many romances. •

One of the most beautifully styled automobiles was the 1914 Stutz Bearcat with Speedster body. The excellently restored bright yellow model shown below is owned by A. J. Koveleski, Scranton, Pa.

Auburn

Art Goebel, first flyer to span the Pacific Ocean, is shown above in his Model 120 Auburn Speedster.

THE Auburn Automobile Company of Auburn, Indiana, was founded in 1900 and folded in 1936. Of its thirty-six-year career the company is best remembered by automobile classicists for the period between the introduction of its first eight-cylinder model in 1925 and its demise in 1936. During these eleven years, Auburn, with modestly priced products, turned out beautifully styled cars, exciting in appearance and often exciting in performance. Though the greatest interest today is in the big V-12s of 1932 through '34 and the supercharged eights of 1935 and '36, Auburn in 1927 gained considerable prestige with its 8-88 model.

Between July 28 and August 7, 1927, two model 8-88 roadsters and one 8-88 sedan set thirty-four new unlimited stock car records for distances from 5 to 15,000 miles. This can be considered quite a feat.

The 8-88 roadsters sold that year for a modest $1,995. They were equipped with 130-inch wheelbase chassis, eight-cylinder L-head Lycoming Model 4HM engines (the same Lycomings were used by Elcar, Gardner and Roamer) of 298.5 cubic-inch piston displacement. The sedan, similarly powered, sold for $2,195.

The 1927 speed tests, supervised by AAA, were run on the Amatol Board Speedway near Atlantic City, New Jersey. Ten days and nights of continuous driving were endured under trying circumstances with rain on nine of the ten nights and heavy fogs during the early morning hours. The sedan completed 2,000 miles at a new record for closed cars of 65.583 mph. One of the roadsters did this distance at a then new record for open cars of 70.084 mph. Road-

ster No. 1, in addition to clocking 76.111 mph for 100 miles, rolled out the 15,000-mile distance at 61.377 mph. Roadster No. 2 completed the first 1,000 miles at a high 72.512 but because of a technicality—no application had been filed in advance for the 1,000-mile distance for this particular car—the performance did not stand as official. This roadster was withdrawn at 12,500 miles with a cracked cylinder block.

Reports of the test gave the Auburn 8-88 sedan a public boost from the standpoint of ruggedness, durability and speed. The thirty-four new records set up by the sedan and the No. 1 roadster made the rest of the automotive industry begin to worry about their laurels. Boss man, Wrigley, was confident that his judgment in hiring dynamic young E. L. Cord, the company's new guiding spirit, was a good one.

The Auburn 8-90 cabriolet of 1928, sold for less than $2,000, had straight eight L-head engine.

In 1930, the 8-125 beat all cars for value. It featured dual manifolds and hydraulic shock absorbers.

Auburn 8-100 Speedster, in 1932, developed 100 hp. The model was one of seven styles available.

Photo courtesy J. A. Wood

Photos above show front and rear view of 1932 twelve-cylinder Auburn Speedster. Note similarity of front fenders to those of Chrysler Custom Imperial's. Rear deck design is beautiful sight for classic car fanciers.

The most expensive Auburn model produced in that record-breaking year was its seven passenger, 4,200-pound sedan, which sold for $2,595. By contrast, a glimpse at the most expensive models of some of its competitors that year is of interest. Cadillac's 138-inch chassis Imperial Suburban was tabbed at $4,350; the Cunningham six-passenger limousine, $8,100; Dupont's convertible sedan was $3,750; Lincoln's seven-passenger limousine was $5,200; the Locomobile collapsible cabriolet in standard version was $7,750; MacFarland's town car, $9,000; Packard's seven-passenger sedan limousine, $5,250; Pierce had a French Landeau for $8,000; Stearns-Knight's seven-passenger limousine listed at $4,950; the Stutz cabriolet town car was $6,895 and Roamer, with the same power plant, was advertised for $3,285.

The first 8-88, Auburn's first eight-cylinder car, was built in 1925. The company continued to make eight-cylinder jobs through the last model in 1936. The 8-88 was a good-looking car with steel spoked wheels, knock-off hubs, four-wheel mechanical brakes, a five-main-bearing crankshaft and in 1928 was introduced for the first time with a sporty two-seater boat-tailed Speedster body. Good styling, engineering and speed achievements during Auburn's last decade were no accident. The company's policies by 1929 were controlled by E. L. Cord, and his organization was responsible not only for the spectacular Auburn V-12 and the blown Models 851 and 852 Auburns, but also the Cords, Duesenbergs and Lycoming Motors. To spark the corporation, some of the industry's top talent was tapped, including designers Alexis de Sakhnoffsky, Gordon Buehrig, Wade Morton, speed merchant Ab Jenkins and Fred and August Duesenberg.

On January 1, 1932, P. P. Willis Corp., Chicago, representing the Auburn Automobile Co., announced the new 1932 Auburn Straight Eight in seven models in both the Standard and Custom lines, including a five-passenger convertible phaeton sedan and two-passenger Speedster. This was the 8-100 model. It featured selective ride shock absorbers, free-wheeling, silent and constant mesh transmission gears, automatic chassis lubrication and a dual ratio Columbia gear. The 8-100 speedster and convertible were both eye-winning models but the big news was its 160-hp V-12 with a 133-inch wheelbase plus all of the features of the Eights.

The Columbia Axle Co., developer of the dual ratio axle, was a division of Cord and hence an associated company of Auburn. Actually the Columbia dual ratio acted as a set of overdrives for each gear.

Chassis of first Auburn V-12 of 1932. Sturdy side rails are Auburn-pioneered X-type construction.

In practice, dual ratio gave the driver of the Auburn V-12 two sets of gear ratios. In the "high" high speed, revolutions of the engine were reduced by one third with the speed remaining the same, while in "low" high speed the car had excellent acceleration with a 4.5:1 ratio. Pre-selection of gear ratio was an additional feature of the device. The driver who anticipated traffic congestion or a possible need of sudden acceleration could switch the dash-mounted control to "low" high. The actual change in gear ratio was delayed until the clutch was depressed which automatically operated the control mechanism. A piston operated by vacuum from the intake manifold took over the mechanical effort of changing position of the sliding dog-type clutches on the axle driveshaft.

In 1933, two more models were added to the Auburn line: the Salon Eights and Twelves. V-shaped, single bar bumpers, dual chrome-plated horns under the headlights, V-ed windshields, a redesigned radiator grille, a fold-down panel type footrest were among the new body features. Motor mounts got rubber cushioning at all four suspension points and the frames were beefed up to give twice the torsional strength of the 1932 design. In general appearance and operation, however, the models were like the '32s but more rigid

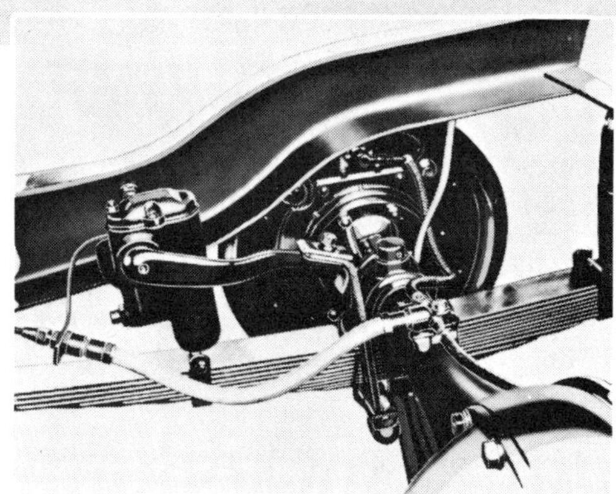

Lovejoy hydraulic shock absorbers were standard equipment of all Auburn 1932 Eights and Twelves.

Front end shows oiling tube to spring bolt and front bumper bracket integral with the frame horn.

Top left. 1932 Auburn 8-100 series custom sedan had 127" wheelbase, dual ratio rear axle and automatic lubrication; $2,500.

The 1934 Custom 8-50, top right, sold for under $2,000 in 1934. Model had 115 hp Lycoming engine, 126" wheelbase chassis.

Left. Artist's conception of the 1935 supercharged Speedster shows advanced streamlining, novel front fender arrangement.

and vibrationless. The cheapest model sold for a surprisingly low $1,245.

Despite the V-12, Auburn was not a large contender in the automotive market during 1932. During the first ten months of '32, its over-all sales were a puny 11,138 models—a drop of 60.3% from its 28,103 sales units during 1931.

The question may be asked why Auburn is an automobile classic when it sold strictly in the lower-middle price brackets. The answer lies primarily in the exceptionally fine body styling. Also, even during the insecure days of 1932 when the V-12 was introduced, Auburn was still hopeful of bettering its position in the industry, and sold the V-12 at a decided loss.

By hindsight, many but-ifs could be used to refer to Auburn's eventual downfall. Generally speaking, despite enthusiastic appreciation of Auburn's top line leaders, those buyers who could afford quality cars usually were affected by price as well as design and engineering. The finest of the Auburns year by year were pegged too cheaply to carry snob appeal. This was coupled with the fact that the quality car purchaser would invariably hesitate to buy a product which had the same name and general appearance of a far cheaper product. In 1935, for example, when the Speedster 851 model was selling for $3,600 and well worth the price, the Auburn Model 653, six-cylinder, five-passenger four-door sedan retailed at less than $800.

In 1934, Auburn dropped the Twelve and for the first time since 1928 failed to produce the Speedster-bodied car. They had lost far too much money on what they had thought would be a real prestige builder. The V-12 Auburn had been launched with the hope of finding the market that the somewhat doggy performing L-29 Cord had failed to find.

Yet in 1935, the company was back to take a beating again. This time with the Auburn Model 851, an eight-cylinder, supercharged job which in Speedster or convertible sedan body types are prized frequently beyond their original cost by classic collectors today.

The Lycoming eight-cylinder supercharged engine developed 150 hp at 2,900 rpm. The un-supercharged versions on the same chassis developed 115 horsepower at 3,500 rpm. The leader of the 851 line was the Gordon Buehrig-designed Speedster. This racy looking job with a tapering fishtail, deeply skirted fenders, no running boards and exposed exhaust stacks was originally intended for a more modest displacement Duesenberg installation. The Speedster's rear deck, unlike that on many of the earlier models, could be raised and the storage space utilized.

Schwitzer-Cummings of Indianapolis

Most popular Auburn of 1935 was the 85 hp, six-cylinder, two-door brougham, selling for only $695.

Priced at under $1,200, the 8-98 convertible phaeton cost less than a third of most of its competitors.

built the water-cooled centrifugal type blower which drove off the timing chain through planetary gearing, giving the central pinion impeller a 6:1 ratio so that when the car was peaking at 3,900 rpm, the supercharger was turning 23,400 rpm. Attached to the dashboard of each of the supercharged Speedsters was a plaque attesting to the exact speed attained in pre-sale road tests. Presumably these tests were all made by Ab Jenkins. No car was released from the factory unless it had peaked at better than 100 mph. The fastest of the models sold for general consumption was tested at 110.8, and one of the cars was driven 1,000 miles at an average 102.77 mph.

In 1936 the model 852 was honestly advertised as the world's fastest stock car, and that year the car broke seventy speed records. In all, approximately 500 of the models 851 and 852 Speedsters were made. There was only a very slight difference between the two models. The 1935 version had narrow pleating in its leather upholstery. In 1936, the 852 used broad, full panel leather with a single seam in the middle rather than pleats.

Though the Auburn has been criticized by some for its ride and road handling characteristics, present-day owners insist that the Speedsters are the most comfortable cars on the road. They consider that the four semi-elliptic springs and the Delco double-acting shocks offer a smooth ride and the large torsion bar stabilizer in the rear permits safer and faster cornering than the average present day Detroit product.

The sale of only 500 Speedsters and an equally modest acceptance of the other models put the Auburn Company finally to the wall in 1936. However, spares are still available today. Dallas Winslow, of Grand Blanc, Michigan, bought up nearly $1,000,000 worth of Auburn, Cord and Duesenberg spares for his A.C.D. Company (the initials stand for Auburn, Cord, Duesenberg) as well as parts for Hollywood Grahams of '40 and '41, Hupmobile, Pierce-Arrow and others. A.C.D. of Auburn, Indiana, is responsible for keeping many twenty-year and older Auburns on the road today. The Auburn, Indiana, outfit supplies anything from a bumper to a complete rebuild job.

Maybe the Auburns weren't very costly in their day, but if you think they were all floss and appearance, just try to stick with a blown Speedster some day on a super highway with your new Detroit job. You won't. •

Model 851 supercharged 1935 phaeton sedan is rarer today than the 851 Speedster, but less sought after by collectors.

1936 Speedster 852. Car can cruise, today, at an effortless 90 mph, with more than 73,000 miles on speedometer.

The last of the Auburns, the '36 supercharged Model 852s held over seventy international speed records.

All Speedsters, from 1928 through '36, showed the same sweeping grace as pictured here on 1931 model.

Cadillac and LaSalle

Always a leader in new ideas, Cadillac introduced the first electric starters and water-cooled V-8s.

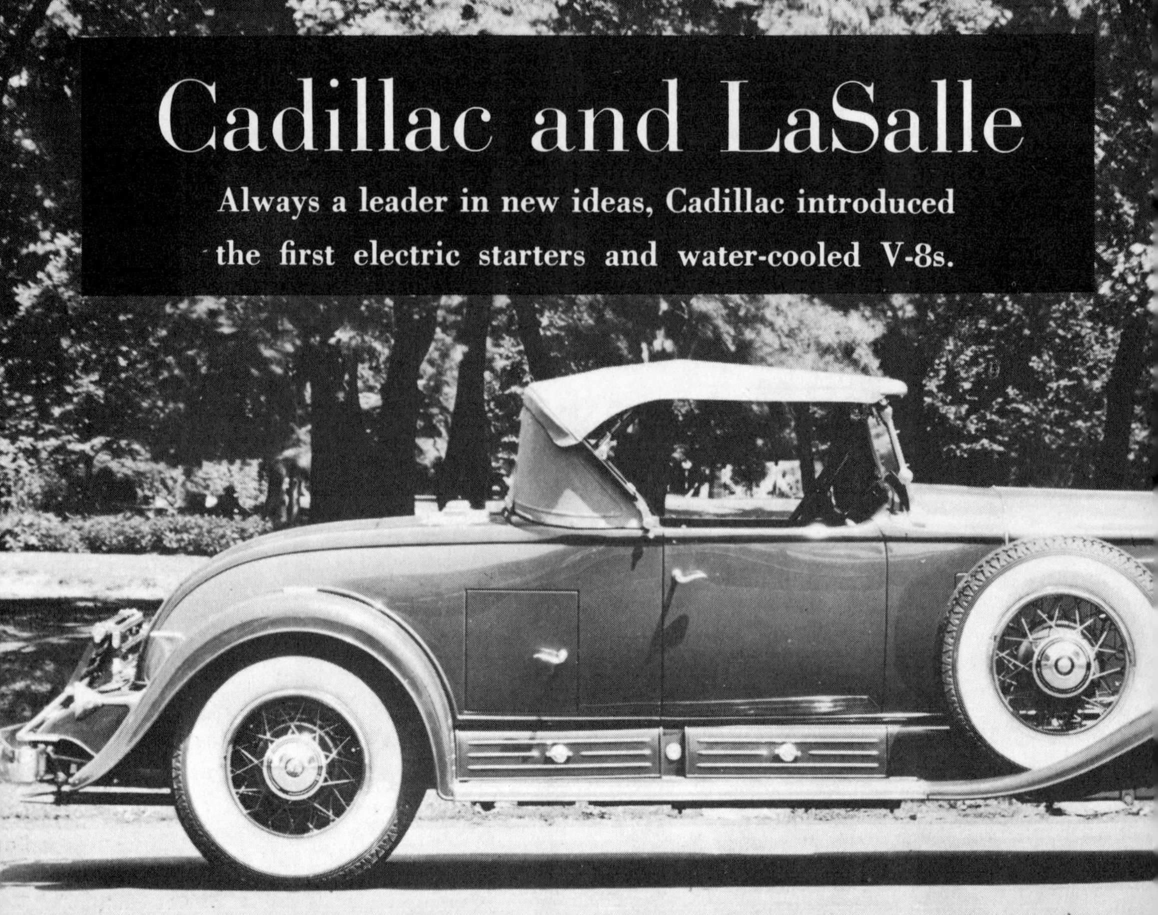

THE Cadillac Automobile Company was organized in 1902 by Detroit financiers, William H. Murphy, Clarence A. Black, A. F. White and Lem W. Bowen, who backed their investment with the mechanical genius of Henry M. Leland. With Leland and Henry Ford as Chief Engineer (of Detroit Automobile Company reorganized as the Cadillac Motor Co.), the first Cadillac, a 6½ hp, single-cylinder o.h.v. job went into production. Leland and Faulconer, early machine tool manufacturers and producers of automobile engines since 1901, (builders for Oldsmobile that year) provided the power plants. Ford left Cadillac the first year of its organization so that Henry Leland was largely responsible for the meticulous workmanship that went into the early cars which gained international fame and their first Sir Thomas Dewar Trophy in 1908, when three models were driven 500 miles each without a single breakdown in English trials under the supervision of the Royal Automobile Club. Such was the precision workmanship in Cadillacs of that period that those three cars were completely dismantled, the parts intermixed and three cars were built from the miscellaneous heap of parts, with no fitting problems.

Throughout automotive's pioneering period, Cadillac was a leader in the adoption of numerous new developments. Among them was the installation of the first electric starter on production models, numerous advances in lighting and ignition, topped by the first production water-cooled V-8 engine in 1915.

In 1917, 74-year-old Henry Leland resigned from the company which had become a division of General Motors in 1910. Cadillac continued to roll on through 1925 with a continually enhanced reputation for a solid, rugged, if not overly distinguished product style-wise. That year, Laurence Fisher, one of the brothers who founded the famous Fisher Body concern, assumed the presidency of G.M.'s Cadillac Division. Fisher's influence on the division became apparent. A larger V-type 8-cyl-

inder engine was introduced for the 1927 Cadillac line which developed 90 hp at 3,000 rpm. This was a 341 cubic-inch, replacing the former 314 job. Rear axle gearing was beefed up as was the differential carrier. Four-bearing support was used on the camshaft; a torque tube drive was adopted to reduce transmission noises. Springs were underslung, contributing to decreased overall height of the car. The driver's seat was made adjustable by means of a crank fitted to the top of the seat back. Prices of the 314 ranged from $2,995 for the five-passenger brougham on 132″ wheelbase to $4,350 for the seven-passenger Imperial Suburban. Prices for the more potent and larger 140″ wheelbase Model 341 were not materially changed although a line of twenty-four body styles was offered.

The big news from the Cadillac division that year was not the Cadillac engine and chassis modifications, but the introduction of a new luxury car, the La Salle, in seven different body styles with a price range of $2,525 to $2,650. Those prices, of course, don't sound overly high today but compare them, for example, with some of the more

The 1931 Cadillac V-16 rumble seat roadster is one of the most desired of all classic autos.

Nearly 20,000 units of this 1920 Cadillac V-8 Series 59 were sold. It has 132″ wheelbase.

Cadillac Series 63 V-8 of 1925 had balance compensators on the crankshaft, four-wheel brakes.

1928 Cadillac town cabriolet, body by Fleetwood, had silver and enamel hardware, broadlace seats.

Photo courtesy W. F. Chapelle

This 1928 dual cowl LaSalle has gray body, black top, red wheels. Note spare tire on front fender.

Photo courtesy W. R. Gage

Model 341-B, 1929 Cadillac sports phaeton has beige and brown body (by Fisher) and black trim.

First V-16 offered to the public was Cadillac's o.h.v. 185 hp of 1930. Photo shows two-passenger coupe.

First of the V-16s launched was the Cadillac seven-passenger Imperial sedan, priced at about $6,000.

V-12 Cadillacs were sold from 1930 through 1937. The two-passenger roadster above is a 1931 model.

modestly priced cars of these days. The Chevrolet two-passenger roadster sold for $525 and the Ford runabout Model T listed at $360. Of course, Lincoln that same year had a $5,200 model and the 131″ wheelbase Stutz cabriolet town car went for $6,895. But despite less expensive price tags than those of rival luxury cars, both the Cadillac and La Salle had a big impact on the upper bracket car buyer. The La Salle was basically a smaller Cadillac with a 303 cubic-inch, 75 hp V-8 engine, but it had a new and exciting facade.

La Salle's designers quite openly copied much of the new job's exterior appearance from Hispano-Suiza; even the name plate —in H-S fashion—had wings sprouting from a coat of arms. Wire wheels gave the model added dash in an era of duller artillery and disk types. Unlike body styling today, the La Salle lines set out quite purposefully to give the model a chunky appearance, with squarish side lines further broken by the uninhibited use of contrasting colors. Double cowl on phaetons had been seen before but seldom in La Salle's modest price range. Cunningham offered them at $6,150, and on the Locomobile they appeared on the Sportif model which carried a price tag of over $8,000. But on the La Salle, a searchlight, double cowl with folding tonneau windshield, pigskin upholstery and dashing appearance were all to be had at well under $3,000.

Basically the same models appeared in 1928 and that year Fisher and Fleetwood bodies were really gone on color designs. The buying public was as crazy about the color creations from "Nature's Studios" of Cadillac and La Salle's body corporations as the copywriters. The Fleetwood Cadillac five-passenger Imperial sedan lyrically boasted fenders, moldings, running gear and roof in "Feather-edge Brown" and body panels in "Paradise Red of the tail of the flashing beauty of the Red Bird of Paradise." The striping of the same model was "Waigiu Yellow and Paradise Red." In 1928, Cadillac's Fleetwood town cabriolet was done in Midnight Blue and Sable.

The 1930 and '31 model La Salles were far less exciting than their predecessors both in color and body styling. In 1933, La Salle sold only 3,350 cars and Cadillac 3,593, contrasted to an industry total of 1,340,988 units. As an attempt to inject new appeal in La Salle, in 1934 the car was given a straight eight power plant of 240.3 cubic inches, which developed 90 horsepower at 3,700 rpm and bodies were completely restyled. Prices of models were slashed to sell from $1,495 and upwards. The Cadillac line was also reduced to start at $2,395 that year. Streamlined lights and fenders and five port hole-like vents gave the La Salle a wholly new but diseased guppy-like look. The economy price tag did boost sales of the model to 4,543 but in a year when the overall market accounted for 1,705,570 units, even this increase was not impressive.

Cadillac, however, in 1930 had made its bid for the big money market by introducing a V-16, the first sixteen to be introduced by an American manufacturer and a real automotive *pièce de résistance*. These models were provided with Fleetwood bodies and in some versions cost over $8,000. Reportedly there were several specials with fine custom interiors whose ultimate price tags ranged as high as $14,000 but no one has come forth with any evidence to establish this claim. Today, one of the most popular and sought after classic sports phaetons is the Fleetwood-bodied V-16 of 1930 through '32 vintage, during

Photo courtesy D. J. Wendling

Beautifully restored 1931 V-12 Fleetwood convertible has yellow body, vacuum booster brakes.

The last of the famous flat radiators was put on this 1932 Cadillac V-12 sports phaeton, above.

which years very few changes were made in the Sixteens.

In 1933, production of the V-16 was limited to 400 cars, each model of which bore a suitably inscribed plate carrying a serial number of 1 to 400. The bodies of the Sixteens that year were only built to order; though sufficient engines had been back logged, the demand never reached within a hundred models of the limitation forecast. The Sixteen had a 3x4″ bore and stroke with 452.8 cubic-inch piston displacement. It developed 165 hp at 3,400 rpm. Its compression ratio was about standard for the era being 5.7:1 with an optional 5.4:1 ratio available. It was also made in either 143″ or 149″ wheelbase. The only passenger cars developing greater horsepower in 1933 were the Duesenberg with its fantastic output for that period of 265 hp at 4,200 rpm, the 490.8 cubic-inch Marmon 16 with 200 hp at 3,400 rpm and Pierce Arrow's 12, developing 175 hp.

Mechanically, one major change occurred with the adoption of independently sprung front wheels on both Cadillac and LaSalle for 1934. Two-way hydraulic shock absorbers were used front and rear, and the ride control —adjustable from the driver's seat— was continued. Both the riding and road handling characteristic of the '34 Cadillacs were improved over predecessor models since the unsprung weight

Series 90 V-16 Cadillac of 1938 had V-ed grille, louvered fenders, was one of the largest cars.

of 460 pounds was reduced by 100 pounds. On all models, the engines were moved forward, which, coupled with lengthened wheelbase, offered far greater passenger room. The V-12 (a 368 cubic-inch 135 hp model) introduced shortly after the V-16 in 1930 had a 146″ wheelbase.

Cadillac in 1935 decreased the compression ratio of the V-12s and V-16s from 6.25:1 to 6:1. La Salle had its compression ratio raised from 6:1 to 6.5:1, picking up 5 horsepower increase from 90 to 95 at 3,600 rpm.

In 1937, the straight eight La Salle motor which was adopted in 1934 was dropped as was the Cadillac V-12, and the La Salle was equipped with a Cadillac V-8 power plant, becoming in essence the cheapest version of the Cadillac. In 1941, when Cadillac's cheapest car under its own label carried a price of only $1,350, La Salle was dropped since it was impossible to produce it at a materially lesser price.

The most desirable of the La Salles today are the 1927, '28 and '29 sports phaeton models, which, as production cars, are considered "compromise, borderline or marginal classics" by the classic purist but are nonetheless in great demand. Though the Cadillac of those two years are also appealing, the more exciting of the classic Cadillacs by far are the V-12s and V-16s of 1930 through '33. •

Resembling the Packards of the same year, the 936 Series 60 convertibles were not impressive.

Above is the very popular 1938 series 75 Cadillac V-8 convertible sedan. Note spare wheel cover.

V-16 limousine was custom finished for the late Senator Glass of Virginia, at a reported $14,000.
Photo courtesy H. D. Chisholm

Chrysler

Since 1924, Walter P. Chrysler's firm has been turning out cars with a justly deserved reputation.

Six-cylinder Model E-80, 92 horsepower chassis, was selected for this custom built, dual cowl 1927 phaeton, with an extra high body silhouette.

IN the past thirty-three years Chrysler has moved from its Model B first automobile, a six-cylinder, 68 hp at 3,200 rpm job, to its 390 horsepowered at 5,200 rpm models. In the present day horsepower race, Chrysler leads the pack. To the automobile classicist, however, Chrysler's greatest years were 1931 through 1933 with a brief but exciting style flurry again in 1939. Its present models, engineering wise, are at or near the top of the automotive heap. But classics of tomorrow have not yet been produced by Chrysler though strong indications are that the new styles—with a returned emphasis on functional design—might present a line of cars which will stir the imagination of a new generation of car lovers.

At present, however, when the classic enthusiast discusses Chrysler, he is thinking of the LeBaron, Waterhouse, Locke and similar creations of the early thirties.

Chrysler has been noted for engineering firsts. Among some of its noteworthy developments or introductions were full pressure lubrication for moderate priced cars, all-steel bodies, rubber insulated steering gear and body mountings, power operated convertible tops, rubber cord spring shackles, exhaust valve inserts, full-flow oil filters, rotary type oil pumps, helical gears throughout transmissions, automatic overdrive transmissions, chair height seats, defroster vents built in below the windshields, safety rim wheels, counter-balanced trunk lids, sway bars, fluid drives, two-tone upholstery and crankshaft vibration dampers of both rubber and steel.

It has been said that the straight eight, 384.84 cubic-inch displacement Chrysler engine with its 3½x5-inch bore and stroke, 125 hp churning a nine main bearing crankshaft, was closely patterned to the Packard straight eight. Whether this is true or not in no way detracts from the enthusiasm of the automobile classicist for the Imperial Custom Eights of the early thirties. Responsible for these cars was one of the automotive industry's most dynamic figures, Walter P. Chrysler.

Chrysler started his contact with machinery at seventeen as a wiper in the Union Pacific Railroad shops. His salary was 7½ cents an hour. By thirty-three he had become Superintendent of motive power of the Chicago Great Western Railway. He wasn't satisfied, however, with a job primarily entailing maintenance. He moved on to the American Locomotive Company in Pittsburgh as its works manager, but despite a key position in railroading he had long been interested in automobiles, viewing them as early as 1906 as the transportation of the future.

When Charles W. Nash, developer of the six-cylinder Buick of 1910, became president and general manager of the General Motors Company in 1912, Nash looked around for a replacement to head up the Buick operation. Walter P. Chrysler was fingered for the job.

Under Chrysler's supervision, Buick production was upped from a meager forty cars a day to more than six hundred a day.

One of the first 1924 Model B's had six cylinders. In Chrysler's first year of sale, 1925, nearly 197,000 of these Fisher-bodied cars were sold.

An Imperial L-80 1928 chassis, with 136″ wheel base was used for this one-of-a-kind convertible sedan. Note the interesting roof attachment.

The builder of this custom landaulet is unknown; chassis was '25 Chrysler Model B, 112¾″ wheel base.

Locke custom-built this basket weave brougham on a 1930 Model CD-8 chassis on 124" wheel base. The engine developed 88 horsepower at 3,400 rpm.

By the time Chrysler left the company in 1920, resigning as president of Buick and vice-president of General Motors, Buick's profits had risen to more than $48,000,000 a year.

Chrysler moved on to Willys-Overland—then in the hooks to a bevy of bankers to the tune of $46,000,000. During his brief stay with Willys-Overland he was able to reduce the debt to $8,000,000 and at the same time established a strong and solvent distributorship for Overland cars.

His work for W-O was interrupted by a frantic call to come to the aid of the Maxwell-Chalmers Company. This veteran outfit was faced with impending bankruptcy with red ledger notations to the amount of more than $30,000,000.

In 1924, when the first Model B Six was launched by Maxwell-Chalmers under Walter P. Chrysler's direction, the new product bearing Chrysler's name got off to a flying start. The B was a mechanical standout due largely to innovations by Chrysler's engineering trio, Carl Breer, Owen Skelton and Fred Zeder. The crankshaft was fitted with seven main bearings and four-wheel hydraulic brakes and steel bodies by Fisher were used. By the end of 1925 when a new model was introduced, more than 100,000 Model B Chryslers were on the road. The new Chryslers had within two years established for their maker a reputation of quality, performance (top speed about 70 mph) and fairly good—but not classic—body styling.

Generally speaking, through 1930 no exceptional factory models of the Chrysler were turned out in six-cylinder version. Yet many an automobile classicist remembers with nostalgia a 1928 two-toned Model 72 roadster or the even flashier dual-colored W-77s of 1930. Then, in 1931, the first of the Chrysler Eights was introduced in Custom Imperial design as a follow-up to the original Chrysler Eights of 1930. As early as 1926—when the E-80, a 92 hp six with 120-inch, 127-inch or 133-inch wheelbase, was launched—Chrysler's sportier line of cars caused comment and unrest among the auto industry's style leaders. The winged capped radiator gave a look of speed which wasn't wholly an illusion. The prestige of the Chryslers was successfully built up on the Continent where the Antwerp branch fostered competition of the E-80 roadsters in Grand Prix touring events. In 1928 a Chrysler Imperial 80-L six took second place in the Belgian Grand Prix, pitted against some of the finest cars in the world engaging in the twenty-four hour grind.

With the introduction of the CD-8 in 1930, Chrysler's prestige was further enhanced. But the prince of the Chrysler line was the Model CG Imperial Custom Eight, the first car of the 384.84 cubic-inch straight eights which developed 125 horsepower. The cars were long in hood with sweeping front fenders, two spare wheels in fender wells. They were most excitingly developed in the Imperial LeBaron phaeton

Extremely rare LeBaron Imperial Custom Eight phaeton. The 1931 automobile is bright red with cream wire wheels and black leather upholstery.

Courtesy Wendling Brothers

One of the most beautiful of Chrysler's custom limousines was the 1932 Imperial Model CL with 145" wheel base. Eight cylinders gave 125 hp.

Custom Imperial Eight, right, was designed by LeBaron. Depending upon extra equipment, the model originally retailed for $3,400 to $3,600.

Courtesy J. O. Goodell

form. The new luxury cars were further improved in styling in 1932 with the Model CL—a 125-hp plant pushing a 145-inch wheelbase chassis, graced by bodies following the Cord and Duesenberg trend of lowered profiles. The first LeBarons on the CL chassis were beautiful to look at but hard to get, since most orders went unfilled for more than six months due to production problems. Unfortunately, the sleek jobs were released before all the bugs had been ironed out. The four-speed transmission was strictly for the birds and almost as rapidly as the cars were delivered they were returned to their dealers with transmission trouble. This wasn't remedied until 1934 by replacing the four-speed transmissions with considerably more reliable three-speed units. Many of the classic Imperial Customs in use today still have the troublesome, unreliable four-speed installations.

Although the displacement of the motor remained unchanged during the IC's span, the added horsepower (from 125 to 135) was gained through a boost of compression

Chrysler Model CP of 1931 on 124" wheel base boasted 100 horsepower at 3,400 rpm, from its eight-cylinder engine of 3¼"x4¼" bore and stroke.

Coach work by LeBaron expresses elegance in every line of this '37 Model C-15 Imperial built on 140" wheel base chassis.

Beautiful cream and light green convertible Victoria has all-aluminum body by Waterhouse. Chassis is a 1931 Custom Imperial.

Courtesy Gordon F. Biehn

Courtesy Thomas Dickinson

After 25 years' service this '32 Chrysler roadster is still in mint condition. Body by LeBaron. Tires are 7.50x17, weight, 4,500 lbs.

Derham, Rosemont, Pa., designed a custom seven-passenger limousine on a 1939 Model C-24 Imperial chassis. Wheel base is 144".

Particularly desirable model is the C-30N 1941 Newport, left. LeBaron styled the gracefully contours of this dual cowl phaeton.

Right. One of the most prized classic roadsters is the 1932 Model CL Chrysler Imperial Custom. Its eight cylinders developed 125 hp.

ratio from its original 5.0:1 to 5.8:1 in 1933. In fact, the same engine in 1935 with 6.5:1 ratio developed 150 hp in the unwanted Imperial Custom Airflow models.

On the tenth anniversary of the first car to bear his name, Walter P. Chrysler introduced his Airflow series. Three Eights and a Six were in the line. The Custom Imperial Eight had been boosted to 145 horsepower by an increase in compression ratio to 6.5:1. The wheelbase remained at 146 inches but the bodies were ten inches wider. Weight was redistributed on the new design. Instead of the normal practice of distributing approximately 40% of the weight on the front axle and 60% on the rear, the new Chrysler was a complete switchabout with 55% of its weight supported by the front wheels and only 45% by the rear. The leaf springs were beefed up and increased nearly a foot in length. There was no question about it—the Airflow's ride was close to the "floating" quality advertised. However, aside from the completely new bodies and a new weight distribution, previously established Chrysler engineering practice was followed. Features such as vacuum operated clutch, free wheeling and silent helical gears in the transmission were continued. But—the car was a dud. Although its body styling, weight distribution and many of its engineering features were to be adopted by postwar manufacturers, the car was a complete failure. In all, only 29,415 of the models were sold in the years 1934 through '37. Airflow models are not considered classics today but are viewed as interesting specimens of a forward step in design concepts.

The most sought after and one of the rarest classics today is the Chrysler Newport phaeton, known as a model C-30N. Only five of the Newport phaetons were built in 1939. The cars combined the newer, smooth flowing lines with dual cowl windshields so dear to auto lovers of the early thirties. The engine was a straight eight with 3¼x4⅞-inch bore and stroke, which developed 140 hp at 3,400 rpm. With only slight modifications, the Newports could turn out 160 horsepower and roll out top speeds of close to 100 mph.

In recent years Chrysler has again turned its attention from stodgy utilitarian lines to more exciting styling in some of its experimental models, such as the K-310, C-200 and D'Elegance with bodies styled by Ghia of Italy. Any of these, had they gone into production would well have joined the "Classics of Tomorrow" parade. Indications are that Chrysler is today once again matching its superb engines with imaginatively designed bodies, something they sadly neglected for several years. •

Cord

Cord offered the utmost in style, comfort and luxury.

During 1929 and 1930, this convertible phaeton sedan selling for $3,295, won thirty-nine Concours d'Elegance in Europe.

WHEN Errett L. Cord of the Auburn Automobile Company, Auburn, Indiana, introduced his first front-wheel drive automobile in 1929, it was neither advertised as, nor was it, America's first front-wheel drive car. J. Walter Christie, in 1904, built the American Christie using this mechanical approach. In 1908, one of Christie's creations was driven to a world's record at 102.8 mph. George B. Selden registered drawings for a front-wheel drive gas combustion automobile in 1879 though the actual working model of the car was not constructed until 1900. In 1918, the Frontmobile made by Camden Motors was displayed at the Grand Central Palace Automobile Show. Even with the demise of the Cord in 1937, the front-wheel principle did not disappear. Today, the rugged and capable Citroen of France still uses a front-drive chassis and has done so since 1933. The ill-fated front-wheel drive Ruxton was announced in May of 1928 and enjoyed a brief flurry in the automotive world. But Cord, with this Model L-29 of 1929, '30 and '31 and the Models 810 and 812 of '36 and '37, was to make the most lasting front-wheel-drive impression on the American automobile public.

All three Cord models are exciting as a piece of engineering design, the latter two models creations of beauty which have withstood the test of nearly two decades and today still attract admiring looks wherever they appear.

The Model L-29 Cord was introduced in 1929. It immediately created tremendous interest, the car being the only wholly different American production car on the market. It was powered by an engine that was well designed though not exceptional. Its Lycoming eight-in-line engine of 3¼x4½″ bore and stroke had a 298.6 cubic-inch piston displacement. The L-29 was offered in a choice of two compression ratios: 5.25:1 or 6.25:1. With the lower standard compression ratio the engine developed 125 hp at 3,600 rpm and had the same engine as the large Auburn Model 120 of 1929.

Wheelbase of the L-29 Cord was 137⅝″. Due to the front-drive principle which eliminated the conventional location of the driveshaft, the L-29 had a lower profile though still offering ample headroom. Most automobiles in 1929 were 70″ or higher from ground to top of roof. Overall height of the Cord was only 61″ (58″ in phaeton version), yet the car had a generous road clearance of 8½″.

Interior fittings were luxurious, with top grade Moroccan leather used in the convertible and fine quality broadcloth in the closed cars. Interior hardware was silver plated. Front seats and steering wheel column were adjustable.

Since relatively few auto enthusiasts have driven front-drive cars, the handling characteristics are not well known. The most important point Cord ads stressed was the distinction of "Having the car pulled instead of pushed." On loose gravel or clay surfaces, the difference between front and rear drive cars was most apparent. Steering control of the front drive is more positive with less tendency to skid or mush since the front wheels pull in the direction they are pointing. With conventional drive, the rear driving wheels push in one direction while the front wheels are pointed in another.

The L-29 did have one minor design drawback which was blown up by its detractors and hurt Cord sales: the engine was located sufficiently far back from the driving wheels so that on exceedingly steep upgrades the front-wheel drive was known to lose traction. As the angle of attack on a hill increased, the focal point of the car's weight was shifted from front to rear wheels, in contrast to a conventional drive car where upgrades tend to improve road adhesion. Actually, however, hills steep enough to produce this situation are very rare.

Other, wholly untrue, rumors persisted in a below-the-belt battle against the new car. One claim was that with front wheel drive, there was a tendency for the front rubber to wear rapidly and blow out. This was patently a lie. Front tires on the Cord wore no faster than those on conventional cars with the same steering geometry and weight. Further, with power to overcome a potential skid, the Cord was actually safer in the event of tire failure.

Despite its many excellent features, the L-29 had been introduced at the most inopportune time of the 1929 stock market crash. The L-29 was not cheap and couldn't rate as utilitarian transportation. In 1930, the L-29's first full sales year, the Auburn 125 (successor to the Auburn 120) in its

In an unusual arrangement, the front axle of the 1929 cabriolet served the purpose of the missing front bumper. Price, $3,295.

Barney Oldfield, left, and Earl Cooper, right, were among racing personnel working for Auburn Co. Insert shows a 1908 racer.

Most original of 44 American cars in '31 was the L-29 Cord. It sold in brougham version for $2,395.

The 1930 front-drive cabriolet was powered by a 125 hp Lycoming eight-in-line, had sporty look.

L-29 power plant included Lycoming straight-eight engine, transmission, differential, clutch, brakes.

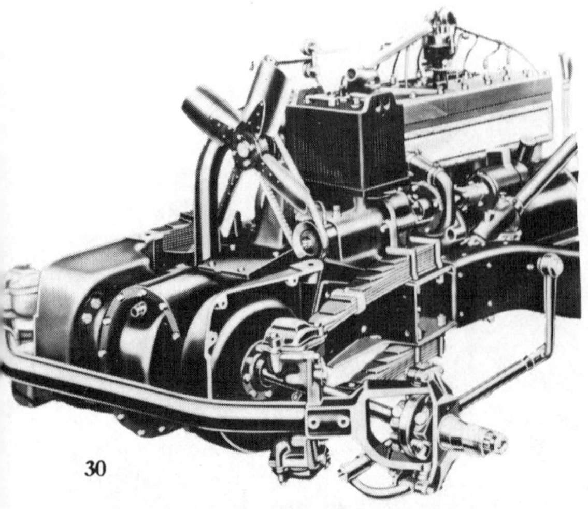

most expensive version sold for only $1,695.

The L-29 was not overly fast, with about 80 mph maximum speed but it could be pushed to over 50 in second gear and could cruise all day at 60. The cars using the highest of the optional gear ratios, 4.076:1, (more commonplace is the 4.418:1) and the higher, 6.25:1 compression ratio heads in some models, clocked better than 90 mph. Gas mileage was in the 12-14 m.p.g. range.

In 1932 when fewer than 340 L-29s sold, Cord dropped production. But Mr. Cord neither considered his front-drive idea a flop nor did he shelve the theory. For three years, as the country wallowed through the Depression, the Cord name was lost to the automotive market. Auburns and Duesenbergs continued to be manufactured—the latter in very limited production.

In 1934, sales of the Auburn Company were less than 5,000 units. This was less than .4% of the total industry sale and the company needed a shot in the arm. Auburn, like others, was scratching for something new or sensational to attract the buying public. As early as 1933, Cord thought the solution might rest with a low-priced Duesenberg.

Gordon Buehrig, of Gotfredsen Motor Body Company—which in the early twenties built bodies for Peerless and Wills St. Claire—moved on to Duesenberg just before 1930 and played a key role in designing the bodies of many of the fabulous Js. In 1934, Buehrig had been transferred from Duesenberg to Auburn where he built a quarter-scale model of the sedan which was to have become the baby Duesenberg and which eventually developed into the Model 810 Cord.

The new Cord 810 was an immediate success. It was by far the most popular and eye appealing creation of the season. Price was quite reasonable, with a range from $1,995 to $2,195 and orders for the new car were brisk. But, unfortunately, the public excitement stirred by its introduction in November waned considerably by the time deliveries started to trickle out of the factory in late spring. The first 810 Cords actually reached customers' hands in March 1936, nearly six months after orders had been placed. The hot enthusiasm had cooled and became less than lukewarm when bugs immediately appeared in the new models.

The first of the 810s steamed like vintage Whites or Stanleys. The radiator area had been miscalculated and was hopelessly inadequate, although this was easily and quickly corrected at no expense to the pur-

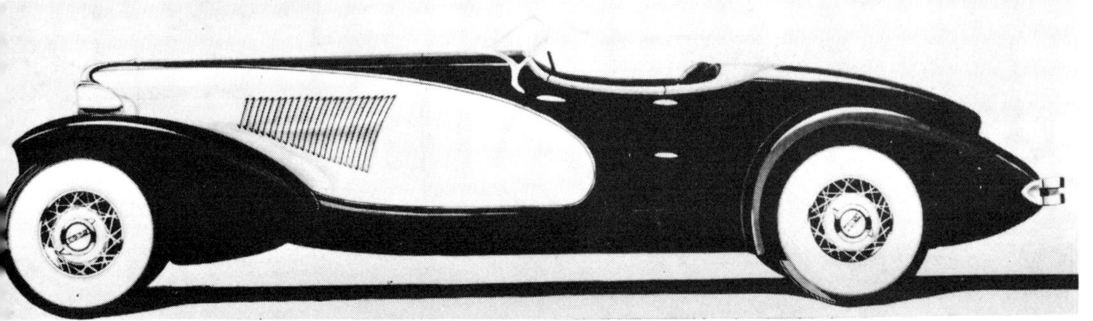

Absence of running boards and faired fenders enhance the low profile of front-drive speedster announced in 1931.

Frederick Thorsen, Portland, Oregon, owns one-of-a-kind 1930 town car, originally built for screen star Dolores Del Rio.

Weyman designed this Elysee model on a Cord L-29 chassis. Car has three-passenger front seat, occasional seat in rear.

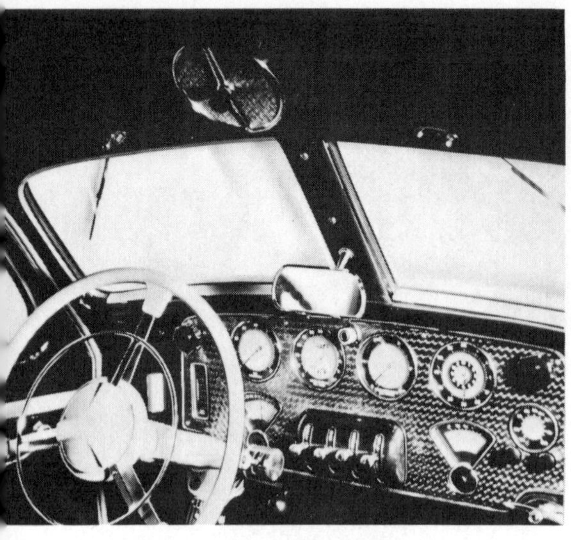

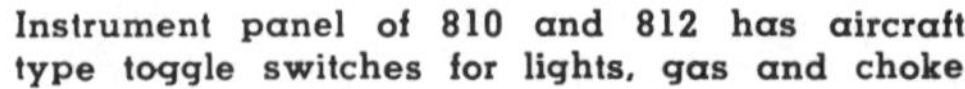
Instrument panel of 810 and 812 has aircraft-type toggle switches for lights, gas and choke.

Handmade prototype of Model 810 had disappearing headlights located on inner side of fenders.

chaser. Another deficiency was in the gear box. The 810s were equipped with a pre-selector shift mechanism and had a habit of kicking out of gear. This, too, was corrected but not until the 810 had chilled most of its early enthusiasts.

The power plant of the 810 was an eight cylinder V-type Lycoming of 3½x3¾″ bore and stroke which at 3,500 rpm developed 125 hp. The compactness of the V made for a far better weight balance than on the L-29 so that the complaint of upgrade traction failure was no longer valid. It moved from 0 to 60 through gears in a shade over 20 seconds. In 1937, the Model 812s (production on these began in late November 1936) could rush from 0 to 60 through gears in about 13 seconds. This, with a pre-selector type shifting mechanism was very quick indeed. The supercharged 812s could top the 100 mark with miles per hour to spare.

Cornering and road handling characteristics of the 810s and 812s were even better than those of the L-29s. They were exciting to drive, quiet, smooth and sumptuously appointed. The front drive offered superior riding comfort as seating in the rear was in front of, rather than above, the rear axle. Yet, after two years of production, only about 2,300 were sold and of these—in spite of the added appeal of supercharging—the 812 sale was under that for the 810. Only 6,725 Cords found buyers in six years of production.

Why did Cord fail? Were they too advanced for their period? The answer isn't an easy one even with hindsight. The public which was so steamed up about the 810 in late 1935, stopped buying the car in early 1937. Surveys indicated that the 1936 buyer viewed the Cord with approval, being impressed both by the car's mechanical features and departures from conventional design and styling. No criticism was directed toward the car's performance once early production flaws were overcome. However, the failure of the Auburn Company to make deliveries when the initial impact of the car was at its peak doubtless had a cumulative effect. Dealers and public alike waited too long and a cooling off period set in. This, plus the early mechanical difficulties gave competition well-needed ammunition.

Cord stood apart from the commonplace, and models which have been restored or kept in condition still offer the driver accustomed to the conventional automobile a thrilling new experience. Without restrictions of any kind, the Cord was designed and built to fulfill one purpose—the utmost in luxurious, exciting transportation. •

Westchester and Beverly sedans used 810 body; more luxurious interior fittings included leather seats.

In 1937, this Model 812 convertible phaeton sedan had a top that disappeared completely into the body.

The utmost in luxury and performance was offered by the supercharged version of the 1937 sedan.

Duesenberg

Described as the "world's finest motor car," the big "D" was guaranteed to outperform and outclass any other automobile on the road.

THE big "Ds" have been tagged with a variety of pet names and descriptive phrases. None, however, has been more apt than the advertising slogan which appeared when the Model A was first introduced: "built to outclass, outrun and outlast any car on the road." Though the Model A, with its eight-cylinder in line, sixteen-valve, 90 hp motor, may not have outrun all other production models, the famed 265 hp Model J described simply as the "world's finest motor car," was just that. The Duesenberg which is today a classic of classics is the Model J or the SJ (a supercharged version that boosted the original 265 hp to 320 at 4,000 rpm).

Despite the vast amount of written material about the Duesenberg, many popular misconceptions persist, among them the fable that Duesenberg was a German car. Nothing could be further from the truth.

True, both Duesenbergs were born in Lippe, Germany—Fred in 1876 and August in 1879—but their widowed mother brought them to the United States in 1880. Neither brother is alive today. Fred, the elder, was killed in a highway accident in 1932 when the Model SJ convertible he was driving to Indianapolis left the road on a slippery curve. August, at 75, died in January 1955 of a heart attack. But the two brothers have loaned their name to an automobile which has stirred the imagination of the American motoring public for thirty years.

In 1905, Fred, who worked as a mechanic in his own garage and frequently raced motorcycles and automobiles, discussed the idea of designing and building a fast, durable car with a Des Moines, Iowa, lawyer named Mason. With Mason's financing the first Duesenberg-built car was marketed

Fred Duesenberg is shown behind the wheel of one of the first SJs, a '32 La Grande phaeton.

in 1906. It bore the name Mason, sold for $1,250 and its twin cylinders developed 24 horsepower. In runabout version it weighed 1,750 pounds.

Through 1909 the Mason continued to be marketed and it established a modest reputation, particularly in hill climb events. F. L. Maytag bought out the company in 1910, shifted its operation to Waterloo, Iowa, and later Detroit, under the name of Maytag-Mason Motor Co.

Fred left Mason in 1910, and in 1911 with August now as a full-time team partner, Fred started work on a new race car which he hoped to qualify for the 1912 Indianapolis Memorial Day classic. The car was only 230 cubic inches, smallest displacement in the entire entry list which ranged upwards to the huge Case Specials of 499 c.i. The four-cylinder Duesenberg design broke a block during pre-race testing and failed to qualify but later, in 1912, it won the Algonquin Hill Climb and turned in a promising performance at several other major racing events.

The Duesenbergs' entry for the "500" in 1912 and again in 1913 carried the name Mason. In 1913, three cars were entered, driven by Bob Evans, Willie Haupt and Jack Tower. These cars were four-cylinder jobs of 350.5 cubic-inch displacement, equipped with Schebler carburetors, which later were to appear again on the early Model Js. Willie Haupt averaged 63.37 mph to finish ninth for the Mason team with Evans going out at the 395-mile mark and Tower lasting only 127.5 miles.

In 1914, the Duesenberg brothers entered two cars. The Duesenberg name was displayed at the "500" for the first time. Eddie Rickenbacker took down tenth place with Willie Haupt finishing thirteenth. Later that season, the then unknown Rickenbacker brought one of Fred and Augie's cars into first spot at three major events. Ralf Mulford, Eddie O'Donnell and Tom Alley qualified three Duesenberg mounts that ran in the International Sweepstakes at Indianapolis in 1915. O'Donnell rolled in to a fifth place finish at 81.47 mph with Tom Alley in eighth.

In October of 1921, the first Model A Duesenberg passenger car was publicly shown. During the initial year of production, the original As were turned out at the Duesenberg plant in Elizabeth, New Jersey. Not until 1922 was the first straight eight

Special body for this 1922 Duesenberg Model A was designed and built by Schutte, Lancaster, Pa.

Courtesy Preston Reed

built by Duesenberg Automobile and Motors Co. at Indianapolis. The Model A was America's first production car straight eight and also the first to be equipped with four-wheel hydraulic brakes. The block was of a four-valve in head design, a variation from the original 24-valve eight. The engine displaced 260 cubic inches with a 2⅞-in. bore and 5-in. stroke, and was only slightly different from those raced the same year at Indianapolis when Roscoe Sarles, Jimmy Murphy, Eddie Miller and Benny Hill carried Duesenberg wings to second, fourth, sixth and eighth spots.

The Model A was available with two styles of chassis, the cheaper listing at $5,000 with the heavier cabriolet costing $7,500. In roadster form the less expensive chassis weighed 3,300 pounds and its 90 hp offered better than average acceleration and an 85 mph top speed. Model As are actually rarer than Js for less than 100 were produced between 1921 and '26 when the model was discontinued.

As early as 1926, hints of the Model J were carried in the press. In early October of that year, E. L. Cord announced the formation of Duesenberg, Inc. At that time Cord was 31 and had already made himself felt in the automotive business when he moved into the Auburn Auto Co. as president two years earlier. When Cord took over Duesenberg, Fred was relieved of managerial responsibility and given the title of Vice-President in charge of Engineering and Experimental Work. Cord instructed Fred to design "the biggest, fastest and most powerful stock automobile the world has ever seen." At this time, the American prestige buyer was purchasing

One of the earliest Model Js was the '29 Derham phaeton, with manually operated double cowling.

One-of-a-kind body designed and built by Fernandez of Paris on a 1931 long wheel base chassis.

Popular formal body style was the 1932 Beverly sedan by Rollston, forerunner of the Twenty Grand.

Brunn Torpedo phaeton was first of supercharged SJs. Gordon Buehrig designed this $19,000 model.

such European cars as Minerva, Bugatti, Rolls-Royce, Bentley, Isotta-Fraschini, Hispano-Suiza and Mercedes-Benz. It was this clientele that Cord planned to tap.

An interim Model X Duesenberg had been produced between the death of the A in 1926 and the birth announcement of the J in late 1928. Less than twenty Xs were made. Their outward appearance was not too unlike the Auburns in seven passenger, enclosed driver seat limousine and sports touring versions. The Model X caused scarcely a ripple of public interest but the announcements of the new J in December of 1928 were of a wholly different, breathtaking vehicle—265 horsepower with a tested speed at Indianapolis of 116 mph—with a four-passenger touring job.

Two wheelbase chassis were available on the '29 Duesenberg J: one 142½ in., the

Above is cockpit view of Brunn-built Torpedo phaeton. Buttons on wheel control lights and gas. Below, 1931 Derham convertible sedan. Only five of these were made at $15,000 each.

Engine compartment of 1933 SJ speedster shows supercharger boosting regular 320 hp to 400 with a blower. Note size of motor.

other 153½ in. The power plant as that in the racing cars was an eight-cylinder in line but with a bore and stroke of 3¾x3¾ in. and a huge piston displacement of 420 cubic inches, the largest straight eight engine to be put into an American production car. Four valves per cylinder were used. The intake valves were 1½ in., the exhaust valves 1⅞ in. in diameter. The valves were shim adjusted to a .025 in. clearance and claims have been made that after 10,000 miles of high speed running, the valve clearance didn't alter more than .022 inch.

How fast was the Model J? Original tests indicated that the car could move from 10 to 80 mph in high gear in 22 seconds and in high gear could accelerate from 5 to 25 mph in 5 seconds.

The chassis of the first J introduced sold for $8,500. This included fenders, bumpers, six wire wheels with the two spares mounted in fender wells and four Delco Remy shock absorbers. A variety of high gear ratios was available from 3.8 to 4.7:1.

Though first shown at the New York Salon in early December, the original models displayed did not have completed chassis and deliveries were not promised until April 1929. Chassis weight ranged from 4,450 pounds on the shortest wheelbase model to as high as 4,700 pounds on the long wheelbase models in the later SJ versions. With custom bodies, the average sports phaeton weighed about 5,200 to 5,400 pounds and broughams, berlines and limousines ranged from 6,500 to 7,000 pounds or better. But regardless of the weight or body style, motorists quickly learned that no one passed a Duesenberg.

An estimated 380 bodies were purchased by Duesenberg from fourteen different coach builders between 1929 and November of 1936 when the cars were last shown at the New York Auto Show. An estimated 486 Model J and SJ chassis were built, starting with engine No. J-101 to J-587. However, it's possible that engine numbers may have been skipped. The outstanding student of Duesenberg lore, J. L. Elbert, in his excellent book, *Duesenberg, the Mightiest American Motor Car,* probably more accurately estimates the complete run at 470.

Most prolific of the body builders was the Walter M. Murphy Co. of Pasadena, Calif., who made approximately 125 of the units. Murphy designs included town cars, convertible roadsters, convertible sedans with broad doors, low silhouette, narrow roof posts and freedom from decorative trim.

The Willoughby Co. of Utica, N. Y., provided about fifty Duesenberg bodies. Derham Body Co., Rosemont, Pa., was represented by about forty versions, while Rollston of New York City is credited with forty bodies, among them the publicized Twenty Grand Torpedo phaeton.

The Union City Body Co. of Indiana, which was controlled by Duesenberg, built more than twenty bodies which were given the name La Grande. Some bodies built by the Weymann American Co., Indianapolis, Brunn and Co. of Buffalo, and A. H. Walker Co., Indianapolis, successor to Weymann, carried the La Grande coachwork label or were referred to as Walker-La Grande or Weymann-La Grande Duesenbergs. Holbrook Company, Hudson, N. Y., was one of the suppliers of the first Duesenberg sedans displayed in 1928, and the company made at least six formal models. LeBaron, which combined the talents of Thomas Hibbard, Raymond Dietrich and Ralph Roberts, accounted for more than thirty models. Hibbard and Darrin built about a dozen custom bodies for Duesenberg before the concern was dissolved in 1931. Bohman and Schwartz built several Duesenbergs and restyled many others. Castagna of Milan, Italy, built some

A popular model was this hard op Rollston sedan which sold or $17,000 on a long wheel ase chassis. Note long hood.

Courtesy Robert T. Born

LeBaron-styled 1931 seven-passenger convertible sedan on standard chassis. The rear seat has its own windshield.

Another 1931 LeBaron-built convertible Model J shows the different designs achieved by this top coach builder.

Only one model of this 1934 La Grande speedster body was constructed. Union City made it, probably Buehrig-designed.

Franay of Paris was the coach builder of the Model J Duesenberg limousine pictured here at a 1931 Concours d'Elegance.

Sleek rear deck design is evident in this 1935 Rollston, supercharged short chassis convertible.

One of the thirty-three bodies made for Duesenberg by LeBaron, Inc., is a double cowled phaeton.

and many other European builders either made or designed substitute bodies for those already provided.

Average price on the Duesenbergs has been estimated at $16,500. The original 1929 chassis price was $8,500 with body prices $3,500 and upwards. The chassis price was boosted to $9,500 in 1931 with the SJ chassis costing $11,750. The cheapest custom body work rose to $4,500 by 1934. Doubtless, the most expensive of the Duesenbergs were those purchased abroad, since their price would reflect transportation, duty and costs involved in replacing dashboard instruments, head lamps, etc.

Today, few of the original Duesenberg purchasers still own their cars. Many of the cars are receiving loving care by those who could not afford $16,000 or more and who, in some instances, keep themselves habitually broke accommodating the nearly insatiable fuel thirst and replacing time worn parts. But maintenance of a Duesenberg even today is not impossible as there are a number of specialists who through long experience with the cars offer first class service. The outstanding of these is probably Jim Hoe of Westport, Connecticut, who has established a reputation of being the leading Duesenberg specialist.

While Fred Duesenberg gathered fame as a designer and engineering genius, August stayed in the shadows. But those who worked with Augie most closely realized what an important part he played in the brothers' team. After Fred's death, August, in the years 1935 through '39, engineered and built the series of special race cars in which Ab Jenkins broke every record he went after. In 1935, for example, with a nearly stock SJ modified to dual carburetion and Rams Horn manifolding, Jenkins averaged 135.47 mph over a period of 24 hours including fuel stops and tire changes every 400 miles. In one hour, Jenkins averaged 153.145 mph during this Salt Flats run.

In 1947, an attempt was made to bring back the beloved Duesenberg. After some initial announcements by Augie and a Chicago financier that the car would be released in modern version, it was learned that the chassis and coachwork could not be produced in keeping with the Duesenberg standards for under $30,000 and the idea was abandoned. •

A formal town car made by Rollston in 1930 on a long wheel base chassis. Note vertical windshield.

One-of-a-kind Bohman and Schwartz body for 1936 SJ convertible, built for the Prince M'Dvani.

A Duesenberg standard factory convertible Victoria came supplied with a body by Rollston.

Lincoln

One of the most desired of the classic Lincolns is the Locke-bodied 1929 Series L touring car.

This 1929 Dietrich convertible Victoria was one of the earliest Lincolns to eliminate sun visor.

Judkins built the body of this series L, 1924 two-passenger convertible coupe, on 136" chassis.

HENRY M. LELAND, with a background of craftsmanship gained in New England firearms factories, moved to Detroit in 1895 where he organized the Leland and Faulconer Manufacturing Co. His first direct contact with the automotive industry came in 1900 when his firm manufactured transmissions for Random E. Olds. From the outset, Leland stressed precision and neatness in all manufacturing processes under his direction. He helped found the Cadillac Motor Car Co., worked as plant manager for General Motors and established the Lincoln Company in 1917.

The first Lincoln was introduced in 1920. It was known as the Series L, which chassis label continued to designate Lincolns through 1930, although a major engine modification occurred in 1928. The first Lincoln, and those designed for a period of twelve years, were powered by 60° V-8s. With the exception of the 1931 Model K V-8, the Leland engines were rated at 90-brake horsepower at a low 2,800 rpm.

The cheapest model Lincoln introduced in 1920 was a $6,000 four-door sedan. The 4,385-pound car had a 357.8 cubic-inch piston displacement, bore and stroke were 3⅜x5 inches with 130-inch and 136-inch wheelbase.

Despite superior engineering, fine workmanship and quality materials put into the Leland Lincoln, the minor depression in 1921 bit hard into luxury market sales and pushed the company into a shaky financial position. In 1922, Ford bought control of Leland's company, but with the stipulation on Leland's part that he be permitted to remain as Lincoln's general manager. Prices were immediately dropped to make the car more competitive; the mechanically unchanged four-door sedan was listed at $4,200, a mark down of $1,800.

The beauty of Leland's eight-cylinder 60° V power plant lay largely in its extreme simplicity of design. Five main bearings supported the crankshaft which, strangely, was not precision balanced until 1928. Two rear gear ratios were available: 4.2:1 and 4.58:1, with the latter normally installed in the heavier 136-inch wheelbase chassis.

In 1923, the first of the Lincoln "Police Flyers" was introduced on the longer wheelbase chassis. Basically, these models were little changed from the 1920 cars, except for the addition of four-wheel brakes which were not to become standard on all Lincolns until 1927.

Though Henry Ford was seeking a prestige car when he bought Lincoln in 1922, he clashed constantly with Leland on the issue of Leland's meticulous and expensive production methods. Henry's son fortunately held a somewhat different viewpoint. Edsel Ford loved the Leland workmanship as much as his father begrudged the use of costlier machining

Courtesy Scott Brobson

Locke-built, 1929 five-passenger sport phaeton Model L, boasts sumptuous white leather upholstery, has been restored to mint condition. Note center deck arrangement and rear seat passenger windshield.

methods. From the inception of Ford's interest in the car, Edsel was Lincoln's champion. It was he who stressed the need for fine custom coachwork.

The first major engine alteration in the Series L occurred in 1928, when the cylinder bore was increased by ⅛ inch and the engine's cubic-inch displacement was boosted to 284. Though the Model L power plant continued to be listed as 90 hp at 2,800 rpm the bigger buckets and balanced crankshaft gained at least 5 horsepower.

Model Ls were neither the fastest nor the most exotic appearing cars, but they were as reliable as a railroad watch. This was quickly recognized by the gangsters, bootleggers and miscellaneous thugs of the thirties whose nocturnal operations called for reliable and rugged transportation. They took to the Leland product as did the Federal Dry agents and other minions of the law. Just how many of gangsterdom's fingered boys had their last rides in the rear seat of a Lincoln has never been estimated, but the turnout of Lincolns at any mobster's funeral gave vivid indication that the underworld chose Lincoln over any other brand, ten to one.

General preference on the part of present day law-abiding collectors is for the 1928 through '30 Model Ls over the earlier L versions. There are some who claim that in 1928 the increased displacement produced a heavier strain on the main bearings and for the first time in eight years engine vibrations were noticeable in a Leland product.

Along with the LeBaron, one of the most desired collectors' items, is the aluminum Locke-bodied sport phaeton—a five- or seven-passenger beauty with rear cowl and windshield. The overall weight of the five-passenger model was 4,950 pounds. Though the car's acceleration was not exciting, once the job got rolling it had endless stamina and could cruise effortlessly at 75 mph all day long. Some of the features of the later Model Ls which included 6.50x20 tires were a built-in air compressor for tire inflation, trouble lights, automatic feed water tank on the radiator, thermostatically controlled louvers plus luxurious leather upholstery and quality carpeting. Yet this handsome sports phaeton of 1929-1930 was one of the least expensive in the Lincoln line, listing at $4,200. At the opposite end of the price bracket was the $7,200 seven-passenger cabriolet brougham, a specialty of the Brunn Coach Builders.

The first break from the Ls occurred in 1931 when the Model K was introduced. This engine had the same bore and stroke as the late Model Ls, and the engine basically was still an L series power plant, but 120 brake horsepower was developed at 2,900 rpm through an increase in com-

By 1930 the 60° V-8 Model L Lincoln had increased in weight and at the same time improved in body styling. Rearward slanting windows, elimination of sun visor gave clean lines to this factory landau.

Greatest radical change from the Series L occurred when, in 1932, Lincoln introduced its first V-12 Model KB. Engine was a 65° V, 447.9 c.i. piston displacement; it developed 150 horsepower at 2,400 rpm.

pression ratio to 5.25:1. Major chassis change was an increase in wheelbase to a single 145-inch chassis equipped with free-wheeling.

In 1925, one of the rarest of the custom-bodied Lincolns was turned out by LeBaron. Two models only were made. These were sufficiently distinctive to warrant mention, since the hood continued unbroken full length to the swept back windshield, a design adopted by many European manufacturers but never previously by an American production car. The piano hinges were secured to the hood with exposed polished rivets in a manner so dear to Rolls-Royce fanciers. Most unique feature, however, of the LeBaron design was the car's low profile, made possible by tunneling the driveshaft through the car and having a stepdown rear seat construction rather than the conventional flat floor, thereby achieving an overall

Brunn cabriolet Type 258 cost $7,200 in 1933, was powered by 150-hp V-12 with 448 c.i. displacement.

The Series KB LeBaron convertible of 1936 had a glass partition between driver's and rear seat.

dropping of the body by at least eight inches without loss of leg room.

The first wholly radical Lincoln change from the original Series L occurred in 1932 when Lincoln's first V-12, Model KB was released. The KBs of 1932 and '33 were identical. The engine type was a 65° V-12 of 3¼x4½-inch bore and stroke, and 447.9 cubic-inch piston displacement which developed 150 hp at 2,400 rpm with a 5.25:1 compression ratio. In 1932, vacuum booster power brakes were introduced for the first time and were continued on the KA and KB models through 1940.

In 1936, the L-type power plant in 385 c.i. version with its 60° V-8 block was continued on the 136-inch wheelbase chassis, renamed the KA, with a list price for the four-door model at a record low for Lincoln of $3,200. The KB V-12s with 145-inch wheelbase listed at $4,300 for the four-passenger phaeton and ranged upward to $7,200 for the five-passenger cabriolet.

The second series KA of 1933 differed from the 1932 KA in that the 60° V-8 was altered to a 67° V-12 plant. The KA 12 had a smaller bore, 3 inches rather than the 3¼-inch bore used on the KB. The cubic-inch displacement was 66.2 inches, less than the larger KB, but with a 5.5:1 compression ratio the Kay turned out a very respectable 125 hp at 3,400 rpm.

In 1934 Lincoln presented two chassis on wheelbases of 136 inches and 145 inches, both fitted out with a somewhat revamped KB engine. The bore was reduced to 3⅛ inches with the stroke remaining the same

Dual windshields and generous wings are part of this handsome 1937 Model KA Lincoln convertible.

Courtesy Roy Baker

The body designer of this one-of-a-kind Model KA roadster is unknown. Car is of early 1937 vintage.

4½ cubic inches. Compression ratio was boosted to 6.4, where it remained through 1940. The cars were offered in three standard body styles and ten custom designs by Brunn, Judkin, Dietrich, Willoughby and LeBaron. Engine modifications included aluminum cylinder heads and aluminum alloy pistons designed to reduce wear.

But economy measures and short-cuts began to creep into the product. A single dry plate clutch replaced the two-disc type dry plate clutch of the earlier KB models. Such items as bearings and connecting rods began to show the effects of quality cut back.

These reductions in quality were relatively minor but they were apparent to the lovers of finely engineered products. The size of the No. 1 crankcase bearing, for example, was reduced in length by ¼ inch and the quality of the bearings themselves was cheapened. Connecting rods were no longer finely polished. More important, the seven main bearing balanced crankshaft was replaced by a four main bearing shaft; and fork and blade rods, which were the pride of the Leland enthusiasts, gave way to cheaper crude forgings.

The Lincolns from '32 through 1940 were by no means bad products, but as the car slipped in quality, it continued to lose ground along with the other American luxury products, most of which failed to ride out the depression years. However, the Leland quality reputation carried Lincoln through the thirties with appeal to those who wanted solidity and dependability. The Lincoln Zephyr introduced in late 1935 has been considered by some as the first successfully designed streamlined car in America, but it never achieved any great affection from automotive enthusiasts since despite its tapering lines and sharp prow-like forward section, a lack of quality of materials, finish and an inferior powerplant were all too apparent.

The greatest enthusiasm, however, to be directed toward any of the Ford products was focused on the Lincoln Continental. The car, design-wise, used the same basic and successful approach used by Cord, *i. e.*, a box-like body with fenders protruding from the forward and rear corners.

In 1941, Continental, unquestionably an automobile classic, was selected by the Museum of Modern Art as one of eight automobiles chosen primarily "for their excellence as works of art," although "no automobile was considered for inclusion unless its mechanical performance met the highest technological standards." There are few who would disagree with the artistic appeal of the Continental. Its low, sleek, clean and unadorned look distinguishes it immediately from the chrome clobbered, hard top and convertible sedan counterparts of a decade later. On a basis of its high technological standard, even the Continental enthusiasts are inclined to agree that the Museum of Modern Art was generous. The Continental's power plant was never satisfying to any truly discriminating auto fan.

Successor to the Model K, the 1940 Continental had beautiful lines but a disappointing engine.

Bottom. The 1948 model was similar to the '40 except for Cord-like grille and more chrome tinsel.

Today, many of the Continental's staunchest advocates blush slightly when they lift the hood and expose a heated up Ford or Mercury substitution. But such is the impact of the rear deck design that several present-day rival automotive designers have stolen the Continental wheel and deck effect. The low squatty car captured the fancy of the car-loving American public; to many, the Continental still represents the ideal design.

Between 1940 and '48 nearly 5,500 Continentals were manufactured but the two postwar year models turned out in '47 and '48 lacked the distinctive eye-catching simplicity of the '40 and '41s. The main objection was to the restyling of the front end, dropping the Zephyr-like knife edge radiator grille for a more Cord-like rounded bow and restyling with chrome tinsel the formerly neat rear fenders. In October 1955, Henry Ford II tried a comeback into the luxury market with a new version, the Continental Mark II; however, it's too early to say if this will be another true classic. Also, the car was discontinued with the 1957 model, which seems to indicate that it was somewhat of a flop.

The collectors' items today are the '40 and '41s, with the greatest yen for the 1941 model. Though the hard top version —the forerunner of the present day hard top convertible—has the cleanest lines, the rag top version is more in demand. A mint condition convertible Continental '41 today is still better gal bait than an XK 120. •

The Continental Mark II was introduced in 1955 and continued through 1957. The car, Lincoln's effort to recapture the luxury market, had 368 c.i. displacement engine with undisclosed horsepower.

Packard

For many years the choice of the world's social elite, ultra-conservative Packard symbolized the quality car.

IN the fall of 1898, James Ward Packard bought a new Winton, built in Cleveland by pioneer automotive producer, Alexander Winton. The car was strictly a yard dog and before Jim Packard rolled out fifteen miles, he was wishing he had a horse. Granted, the early tiller-steered one lunger was only the twelfth model Winton had made, but Packard, who was a manufacturer of electric lighting supplies in Warren, Ohio, was more than unimpressed by the Winton's performance—he was downright disgusted and had no hesitancy about expressing his critical analysis of the Winton to Alexander in person. Had it not been for Winton's heated response, "Why don't you build a car yourself, if you're so smart, Mr. Packard," some of America's finest of automobiles might never have been developed.

Jim Packard, along with his brother Bill Dowd Packard, took up Winton's challenge. Just before the end of 1899, the first single-cylinder, 12-hp Packard, complete with a three-speed transmission, made its appearance. George Weiss, a garage operator and one-time employee of Winton, worked with the Packard Brothers on their original design. In the fall of 1900, when the new Packard Automobile Co. was incorporated, George Weiss was appointed the company's vice-president.

At the first New York Automobile Show at Madison Square Garden in November of 1900, Packard was off to a good start when they took orders for three cars. To add prestige to the new Packards, two of the three were purchased by William Rockefeller.

Though Packard's first few production models were successful, much credit for the ultimate growth of Packard rests with Henry B. Joy, who bought a Packard in 1902. He was so enthusiastic about its reliable functioning in contrast to other cars that he persuaded a group of his friends to join him in financing a new Packard factory to be set up in Detroit. James Ward Packard agreed to go to Detroit to manage the new plant with the proviso that he be permitted to build the kind of car he would like to drive. In 1903, the same year that Tom Fetch, Packard's shop foreman, made his historic

Courtesy Long Island Automotive Museum

The brain child of Jesse G. Vincent, this 1915 Packard Twin Six was an automotive sensation.

Beautiful styling made this coupe-roadster, 142" wheel base Packard Twelve a standout in 1933.

Nostalgic memories are recalled with this 1925 Straight Eight roadster; engine developed 84 hp.

mud-slogging San Francisco to New York 3,500-mile canter in a one-lunger Packard, later named "Old Pacific," the shift of the Packard Co. to Detroit was made. During the first year of production, Packard turned out approximately 200 model K four-cylinder, side-entrance, touring cars. Though the models sold readily, their $3,000 price resulted in a net operating loss of nearly $200,000 that first year. Had it not been for the financial backing of Henry Joy and his group of wealthy Detroiters—who were willing to dig into their bankrolls for additional funds to move into 1905—the Packard Co. would have folded on the spot.

Quality workmanship, reliability and advanced design were the principal characteristics that caused Packard to rapidly establish a reputation for a fine product.

By 1910, the Packard Co. was running well in the black and Henry Joy grew tired of an operation which no longer offered him a challenge. Alvan Macauley was hired that year as general manager. He brought along with him Jesse G. Vincent, who was to become one of the most

Photo shows Director of the Classic Car Club of America, Edward C. Kavenagh, with '30 Model 733.

Model 734 phaeton, custom built by Packard, had 134½" wheel base, straight eight engine, 106 hp.

Privacy, lush interiors, ample head room were all characteristic of the 1930 Packards. The engine was a straight eight, developing over 120 horsepower.

The Brewster custom sedan limousine was more conservative than the 1930 factory models. Note elegant wooden spoked wheels.

brilliant engineers in the automobile field and who, in 1910, took over as Packard's chief engineer. Under Vincent's direction, at a time when most automotive producers were still arguing about whether the fours weren't just as good as the sixes, Vincent was at work on a design for a V-12, which was first launched in 1915. This original Twin Six was the first of the Packards that was destined to stir the imaginations of four-wheel romantics and the model was to become Packard's first automobile classic.

The Vincent masterpiece was radical in many respects. It was the pioneer American twelve, a 60°, V-12 with two banks of six cylinders each. It also pioneered in America the use of aluminum pistons; the engine that produced the 85 hp at 3,000 rpm weighed 900 pounds.

The veteran classic status of the 1915 series Twin Six was based largely on the narrow angle V-engine's new standard of smoothness and silence among the American production models of its time. The power plant, displacement-wise, was not overly large for its period, the cylinder bores measuring only 3 inches in diameter. But the car could idle down to 3 mph in high gear and roll at that speed steadily. Its acceleration from this extremely low idling point in high to 30 mph without changing gears is reported to have been accomplished within 12 seconds. It could also pound out an honest 80 mph which in 1915 was close to flying.

The Twin Six was as rugged as it was smooth. Its use in mapping out and inspecting the then new, partially complete coast-to-coast highway proved its durability. Henry B. Joy, president of the Lincoln Highway Association, with A. F. Bement, vice-president of the project, averaged 12.5 mph for the 2,700 mile distance from Detroit to San Francisco in 1915 with much of the route in hub-deep mud.

The introduction of the Twin Six was one of the all-time sensations of the automotive industry. The news was flashed on the New York Stock Exchange ticker. The Manhattan Packard showrooms kept their sales staff on day and night shifts as vast crowds thronged the establishment. On the West Coast when the first Twin Six went on display in San Francisco, reports listed 25,000 in line the first two days to see the new marvel as "flawless as a Damascus sword."

A special racing version of the first Twin

A rare sight today is this 1930 long-hooded convertible with body by Dietrich. The clean lines of car are typical of this designer.

Outstanding in style, excellent in performance was this 1931 custom built Model 840 Packard. Note unusual rear deck design.

Favorite of most classic fanciers is the 1933 Packard Super Eight dual cowl sport phaeton.

Courtesy W. F. Chapelle

Six was turned out by Vincent in 1915. With its engine weight reduced by nearly 100 pounds, higher compression ratio and modified carburetion, it produced 110 hp at 3,000 rpm. With this V-12, Ralph DePalma established a number of track records.

Twin Sixes were the cars of the social elite and prominent people of that era. The Packard prestige was not limited solely to the United States. Czar Nicholas II of Russia had a Twin Six, as did the Grand Duke Michael, the Czar's brother. His Highness, the Maharajadhiray Sri Sweai Maharaj Veeranda Shiromani Dea of Alwar, India, owned several. Viscount Jellicoe, Governor-General of New Zealand, selected a Twin Six tourer as his official conveyance. From 1915 to 1923 few cars rivaled the Packard Twin Six.

Standard factory models in themselves had great prestige value, but individual designs by Rubay, Fleetwood, Graff, Derham and others gave added luster to the pride of possessing the "car of unchanging character."

The next major classic mile post in Packard's history was its introduction in 1923 of a Straight Eight, which from the outset proved to be one of the smoothest functioning power plants to come off a production line. This time Packard was not an innovator, for Duesenberg had already pioneered the eight-cylinder-in-line design in America. The Eight of 1923, which carried its crankshaft on nine main bearings also had four-wheel brakes.

During the twenties Packard's solid reputation continued to grow. Its profits were high and this was based on one factor which also had gone a long way toward giving Packard its sound, conservative reputation: models didn't change every year. Packard at that time made capital of this point by playing up the fact that, "a new model would not retain its smartness for only a few months but would keep its identity unchanged for many years to come." Body styling in general was restrained. Square boxishness gave the cars a look of dignity rather than grace. Roofs were high so a passenger could wear a top hat with ease.

As Packard moved into the thirties and the depression years, competition in both the low and high priced market increased. The less expensive cars were vastly improved. Other quality automobiles began to crowd Packard in the upper price bracket. From a peak production year in 1928 of 50,000 cars and a profit in the neighborhood of $25,000,000, Packard's sales began to slump. In 1930, the year after the stock market crash, Packard began to feel the bite as its production dropped to 28,000, and skidded to less than half that figure in 1931. For the first time since Henry Joy and his partners had dropped a quarter of a million back in 1904, the company showed an operating loss.

The year 1932 was even more grim with total production barely topping 8,000 units and this despite the introduc-

In 1932 Packard introduced a new Twin Six, forerunner of the Twelves made through 1939.

tion of a new, under-$2,000 Light Eight. The market for the luxury cars had nearly disappeared. Stutz, Pierce-Arrow and Duesenberg were already on the skids. But Packard wasn't licked. A major change took place in 1934: Packard turned its attention to the cheap car market.

In 1935, the new Packard 120 was introduced. The car was equipped with a small straight eight and was designed to appeal to the man with a $1,000 car budget. Nearly 50,000 of the small Eights did hold that appeal the first year. The senior lines of the Packard, the 150-hp Super Eight and the new 175-hp Twin Six (Packard's most powerful production model to that date) became secondary models to the cost-conscious car buyer.

The automobile classicist sneers at the 120s and the Toy Sixes (as he terms them) and gives them less consideration than the pre-1923 Sixes. Probably most highly prized among the Packard classics are the Twelves. With these cars, in the thirties, came the Packard Certificate of Approval, comparable to a diploma of mechanical excellence. No Packard Twelve owner ever had to break in a new car. In addition to the hundreds of factory inspections, every Packard Twelve was given a full 250 miles of running in and tuning at the Packard Proving Ground, which includes a 2½-mile high-banked concrete speedway, in addition to miles of steep grades, sharp descents and test roads.

A quick look at some of the features of the Packard Twelve of 1933 will establish

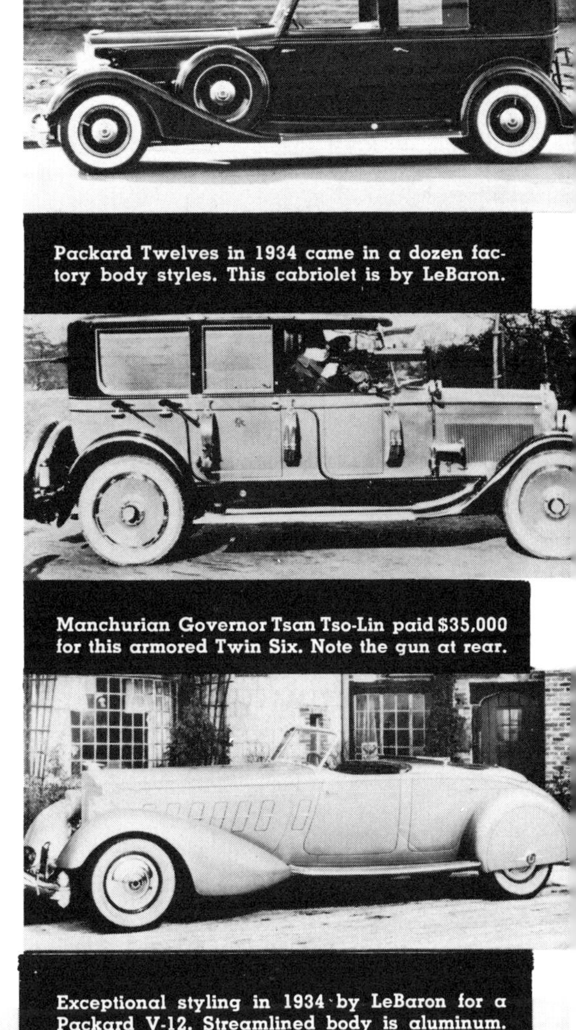

Packard Twelves in 1934 came in a dozen factory body styles. This cabriolet is by LeBaron.

Manchurian Governor Tsan Tso-Lin paid $35,000 for this armored Twin Six. Note the gun at rear.

Exceptional styling in 1934 by LeBaron for a Packard V-12. Streamlined body is aluminum.

Only 781 Packard Twelves were built in 1935. Custom models, above, ranged as high as $10,000.

Courtesy Allen Hudson

Seven-passenger series Twelve touring car, by Dietrich, was used in parades by Franklin D. Roosevelt.

the quality that went into the products. A dashboard, knob-operated ride control permitted the driver to adjust shock absorbers for varying road and load conditions. A fully automatic chassis lubricating system gave a constant supply of grease to all points and automatically fed lubrication to the clutch bearings. A vacuum booster offered power braking, with a dashboard selector to give four degrees of brake pressure. The power plant was conservatively rated at 160 hp.

During the thirties, through 1939 when the last of the Twelves was manufactured, only 5,298 of these masterpieces were turned out in all body styles. This compares somewhat unfavorably to the more than 35,000 Twin Sixes sold from the time of their introduction in 1915 through 1923. Many collectors wonder if there is any basic difference in the power plants of the 1933 through '39 Packard Twelves. The answer is yes. In 1933 and 1934, the stroke was 4 inches. This coupled with a bore of $3\frac{7}{16}$ inches gave a cubic-inch displacement of 445.89 and the power plants were rated at 160 hp at 3,200 rpm. In 1935, this displacement was increased to 473 c.i. by increasing the stroke to 4¼ inches and the brake horsepower at 3,200 rpm was boosted to 175.

Some automobile classic fanciers feel that the Darrin-designed 1940 Packard Super Eights were the finest to carry the Packard name. That point I won't argue. But even Darrin couldn't do much with the 1942 Super Eight Custom 180s which were clobbered up like Christmas trees with an excess of chrome. The 148-inch wheelbase LeBaron limousines also gave a blatant warning that Packard's day in the classic sun was over—at least temporarily. •

Massive grace of this 1937 custom brougham seems to be partially destroyed by bulging front fenders. Windows, however, are neat.

Custom Twelve all-weather cabriolet has LeBaron body. Front design, not typical of the famous designer, has bulky, awkward style.

The 1938 model lacked the grace of the '37s but is nevertheless considered an outstanding example of mechanical smoothness.

Original design by Darrin of 1940 Super Eight was listed at $6,900, is considered by many the most beautiful of all Packards.

Pierce-Arrow

This expensive luxury car was among the finest ever to grace American highways.

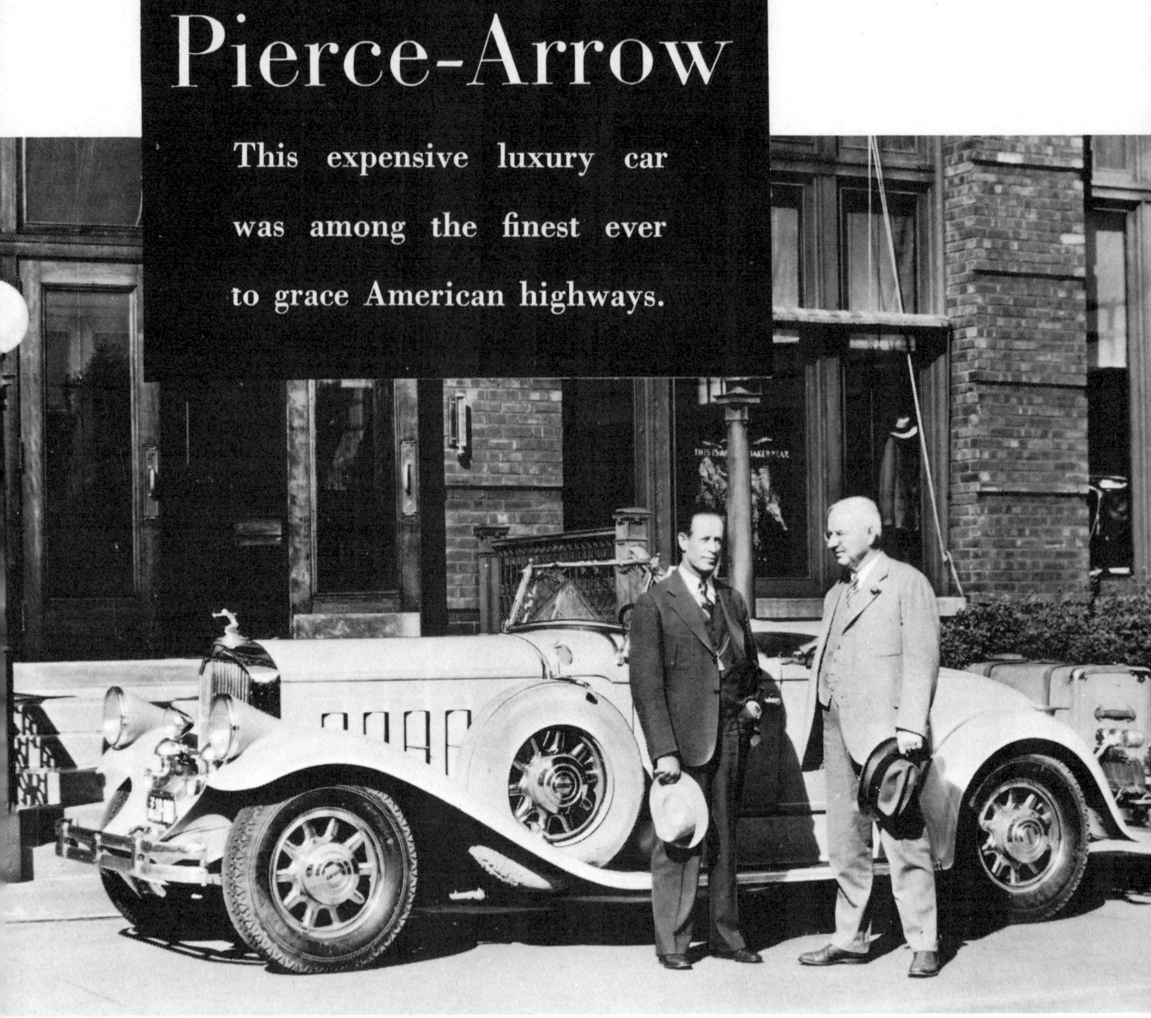

Famous Auto Racer Ab Jenkins, left, drove this 12-cylinder fully equipped Pierce-Arrow roadster for twenty-four hours at a remarkable speed of 112.91 mph on the Bonneville Salt Flats, Utah, in 1932.

PIERCE-ARROW, one of the three big Ps of American motoring, was the last of the group—Packard, Peerless and Pierce-Arrow—to enter the motoring scene in 1901. The big P-As continued to grace American highways until the greatly reduced assets of the Buffalo concern were auctioned off on May 12, 1938, bringing a puny $40,000.

George N. Pierce, founder of the company had been a successful manufacturer of bicycles and bird cages at Buffalo, New York, prior to his entry into the automotive market in 1901 with the Pierce Motorette, a single cylinder, tiller-steered open two seater, powered by a 2¾-hp French-designed De Dion engine.

In 1903, Pierce's Motorette included the first steering post gear shift and a domestically designed and built power plant. In 1904 Pierce introduced his famed Great Arrow, a four-cylinder, 24-hp high seated job with a Panhard-type progressive transmission that was to be retained until 1909. Pierce's son, Percy, entered a Great Arrow in the 1905 Glidden Tour, 860 miles of rough roads designed to shake to pieces all but the most durable vehicle. His entry easily outclassed twenty-two other contestants, and the win firmly established George Pierce's product.

The first Pierce product to carry the name Pierce-Arrow was released in 1909. In 1914 the 60-hp six-cylinder 147-in. wheelbase Pierce-Arrows ranged in price from $5,850 to $7,250. Many people think that the Model 66 Pierce-Arrow was underrated by its manufacturer. The T-head engine, which was claimed to develop 60 hp at 856 rpm, at 1500 rpm could readily turn out 100 bhp, but Pierce conservatively stuck to the lesser figure in its ads.

Though Pierce during its first decade was a leader in innovations and design development, the company after World War I lagged in progressive ideas, rested on past reputation and only advertised its products in a modest manner. After the war, many of Pierce's quality competitors had advanced to eight and twelve-cylinder models. Pierce-Arrow met this challenge belatedly and with questionable ammunition in 1918 with the introduction of its dual valve six. This was a powerful enough job for the time, being able to lug the big chassis smoothly in high gear through a range from 3 to better than 75 mph. But the buying public went for the magic in the sound of multiple cylinders and reasoned that if one could get a V or an eight-in-line car bearing an equally high prestige name, why buy a mere six.

In 1920, Pierce finally shifted the steering wheel from the right to the left side in conformance with the standards adopted years before by most other manufacturers. The P-A added four-wheel brakes in 1924. But little was done about the power plant and business continued to slump.

In 1925, the company, which had based its foundation on quality products at quality prices,. made a tentative attempt to move into the lower priced field in order to recoup its lost market with a 130-in. wheelbase car powered by a 70-hp 289 c.i. displacement six. This model known as the Series 80 had price tags ranging from $2,750 to over $4,000. It was neither priced low enough to appeal to the purchaser of cheaper cars nor expensive and lavish enough to be attractive to the snob value buyer. In August of 1928, Pierce-Arrow's directors and stockholders accepted financing from Albert R. Erskine, president of the Studebaker Corp. Pierce-Arrow, though retaining its identity, became a subsidiary of Studebaker.

Under Erskine's influence, Pierce-Arrow finally switched from its nearly ten-year-old dual valve six to a straight eight. This first eight, known as a Series 81, was originally introduced as a 366 c.i. power plant. Though it was well engineered, it contained no really new outstanding features.

But in 1932, at its lowest ebb in its history, Pierce-Arrow daringly introduced two new V-12s and continued to carry a Series 81B straight eight. For the first time in several years, it looked as though the company could face an operational year in the black. They employed Ab Jenkins to prove the worth of the new Twelve. In the late summer of 1932, Jenkins along with several plant engineers took a stock V-12 P-A roadster to Utah's salt flats. Jenkins drove the roadster for twenty-four straight hours at an unprecedented average speed of 112.91 mph, an impressive 11.2 miles-per-hour faster than the 500-mile Indianapolis record average at that time.

British Racing Driver Kaye Don, posed with 1931 Series 81A eight cylinder-in-line limousine, above.

Rated at 66 hp, the 1917 P-A gave appearance of luxury and ruggedness; its quality was a byword.

The Model 1255 Pierce-Arrow, above, was listed at $6,500 in 1935, in town brougham version.

Below, only known existing model of fabulous 1933 Silver Arrow has V-12 engine. Price, $10,000.

Courtesy Long Island Automotive Museum

At the 1933 auto shows, the most outstanding single model to be displayed was Pierce-Arrow's $10,000 Silver Arrow. With the V-12 already proved, designer Phil Wright had been called in to create a super streamlined car to spearhead Pierce-Arrow's 1934 advertising and promotional plans. Despite an ultimate weight of well over 5,000 pounds, the rakish Silver Arrow was reported to be capable of nearly 120 mph on the straightaway. The power plant was probably one of the finest of the Twelves developed. Designed for long and rugged use, its crankshaft was mounted in seven main bearings rather than in three as was Cadillac's and Packard's.

In 1933 Ab Jenkins increased his stock Pierce-Arrow speed run average to 118 mph for a 25½ hour run. But as any classic car fan knows, quality workmanship and outstanding performance didn't sell automobiles in the mid '30s; hence the rarity of good classics today. In 1934, dealers folded right and left and Pierce-Arrow sales continued to slump. And this in spite of Ab Jenkins, who in a final bid for Pierce-Arrow speed supremacy, averaged 127 mph for twenty-four hours in late 1934, with a modified stock version.

Too late, in 1937, when Pierce-Arrow had already slipped into the early stages of rigor mortis, they announced that they would enter the modest priced field with cars carrying price tags as low as $700. Optimistically, they announced that at least 25,000 of the cheap models would be launched in 1938. No '38 models ever made their appearance and the company's plant and tools were finally sold at auction.

Though production of the Eights and Twelves of the thirties were in limited numbers, collectors planning to restore any of these beauties may be encouraged to know that Atlantic Auto and Truck Sales of 19020 South Figuera Street, Gardena, California, stocks Pierce-Arrow parts. •

Pierce-Arrow 5-passenger Club Sedan, Model 1247, sold for $4,400 in 1935, has L-head 12-cyl. engine.

Headlights in fenders keynoted P-A styling, as shown in this frontal view of Roy Barr Model 836.

Courtesy F. Robert Greene

Clean, classic lines are evident in the sports phaeton, which retained vertical grille in 1931.

Below, in 1936 Pierce was close to end of its days, but models retained their elegant looks.

American Classic Panorama

The names of many of these fine automobiles are remembered today only by a few real enthusiasts.

THE bulk of the automobiles most admired by the purist classic fancier are the super-powered, ultra-expensive custom-bodied creations of the early '30s. Some of these cars, like Cord and Auburn, are most admired from a styling standpoint. Others, like Marmon, are remembered for their superlative engines. And a few like Duesenberg J, KB Lincoln or the Packard Twin Sixes are coveted for both their power plants and body work. Some, like the DuPont, are remembered for their famous name which added a prestige to an automobile that did not wholly deserve it, although the DuPont LeMans speedster, to mention one, is today a valued collector's item. But while these luxury models were scrapping for limited business in the '30s, some long remembered producers of automobiles had already passed from the automotive picture about the time of the late twenties financial crash.

There were those manufacturers whose products mimicked the body styling of Rolls-Royce, at least with a limited number of models. Kenworthy, for example, with its four-cylinder Duesenberg-designed engine, Moon with a Continental six or Roamer, which also had a Continental. All of these disappeared from the automotive scene by 1930 but each, at least in a few models, unsuccessfully aped the R.R.'s styling.

There are many who think back with fondness of the products of Templar Motors Corp. of Cleveland, Ohio. They re-

Courtesy H. D. Chisholm

A rare classic today is this sporty little Templar of 1929 vintage, with hand hammered aluminum body.

Above is Merrimac-bodied 1929 Model G DuPont touring car. Note the neat folding top arrangement.

Buffalo wire wheels plus yellow and black paint job gave the 1928 DuPont sport phaeton distinctive look.

member the touring roadster at the turn of the century with its hand-hammered aluminum body, two spare wire wheels mounted one above the other in a well sunk in the rear deck. There were no doors on the Templar and an aluminum step mounted on the outside of the body with its embossed leather cuff pad gave access to the neatly molded individual seat cockpit. The windshield of cast bronze was pitched at a rakish angle and the overall effect was smart and sprightly. Incongruously, standard equipment included an autographic 1A Junior folding Kodak—or was that supplied for candid pix of dates clambering aboard? The Templar was light, flexible and though its four-cylinder overhead-valve engine turned out only 43 hp at 2,100 rpm, it could reach a top speed of 60-65 mph with better than average acceleration. The model sold for $2,635 and the claim for the 118-inch wheelbase car as the "superfine small car" was an undervaluation if anything.

When the name Cunningham is mentioned today, the sports car enthusiast immediately thinks of Briggs Cunningham and his contemporary, superbly designed combination of Italian-styled bodies and modified American stock power plants, which have successfully competed at Le Mans. However, to the automobile classicist, the name means James Cunningham, Son & Co., Carriage Builders, which firm originally set up business in Rochester in 1838, and in 1849 turned out everything

Volney Lacey designed the 442 c.i. V-8 power plant housed in this 1920 Cunningham speedster.

Cunningham designed and built their own bodies. In 1925, 100 models of the roadster were made.

from sleighs and dogcarts to hearses and ambulances. James Cunningham was among the pioneers to gauge the trend from horse-drawn to motor vehicles. Before the turn of the century, the first Cunningham electrics were made and in 1907 the company switched to internal combustion engines for their horseless carriages. By 1910, Cunningham was making its own power plant, a four-cylinder job, and in 1911 a Cunningham was selected to lead the Glidden Tour as the officials' car.

Unfortunately, the Cunningham's driver lost control while traveling at high speed; the car left the road and the Chairman of the American Automobile Association, Samuel F. Butler, was killed. The Race Referee, his wife and the driver suffered serious injuries and the resultant publicity was extremely poor, to say the least.

Cunningham's later solid reputation was largely built around a V-8 designed engine of 441.7 cubic-inch displacement, created by Volney-Lacy. Cunninghams never reached the market in volume for the bodies were custom built and the chassis largely hand made in estimated quantities of 100 units, or less, each year. The Lacy-designed motor was to change only slightly through 1931 when the final chassis was made. But the cars which ranged in price from $6,000 to $15,000 with an average cost of about $7,500, appealed to the wealthy connoisseurs of the twenties.

Even within recent years, owners of thirty-year-old and even more ancient Cunninghams have their chauffeurs drive to the Rochester plant to pick up spare parts and give the American equivalent of the Rolls-Royce a general tuning. The company, today, is in business as a manufacturer of garden tractors.

Marmon, during three decades of manufacturing automobiles (1902-1933) produced three outstanding models. The first of these was the four-cylinder Model 32, 1909 through 1914. Though the 1911 Ray Harroun Indianapolis-winning Marmon Wasp was a six-cylinder, the engine was based on the Model 32 design and the prestige gained by Marmon as a result of Harroun's win was particularly helpful.

In 1916, Marmon switched to its six-cylinder Model 34, a 339.63 c.i. engine that developed 74 hp at 2,450 rpm. Though the wheelbase of the 34 was a generous 136 inches, the seven-passenger touring car weighed only 3,295 pounds ready for shipment. Aluminum was extensively used. Body, fenders, hood, radiator shell, main structural member of the motor and many smaller castings were all aluminum. Motor lubrication was achieved by the famed Marmon hollow crankshaft forced feed system, supplemented by a hollow rocker arm pivot so that all valve parts were lubricated by pressure feed. This model, exceedingly popular in post-War I days, was basically unchanged until 1924.

In 1927, three Eights were introduced: Model 869 of 211.2 cubic-inch displacement, an 879 of 303.2 c.i. and the Big Eight of 315.2 c.i. displacement. All three of the Eights were of lesser displacement than the Model 34 six-cylinder engine. An interim 1926-27 model "Little Marmon" Eight of 190 c.i. and 116-inch wheelbase, selling under $2,000, proved to be a dud.

Neither the bodies nor the power plants of the Marmon Eights were overly distinguished, but the Marmon V-16 first introduced publicly in 1931 was something else again. The power plant won for its designer, Howard Marmon, the Society of Automotive Engineers' award as the finest design in 1931.

Courtesy A. G. Rippey

1931 Marmon V-16. Its 490.8 c.i. engine, 200 hp, is considered one of finest power plants ever.

Courtesy Edmund L. Robinson

Only 58 of the approximately 850 Marmon Sixteens are known to exist today. Above is a 1932 model.

Underhood view of Marmon V-16 power plant shows polished aluminum and chrome plated steel.

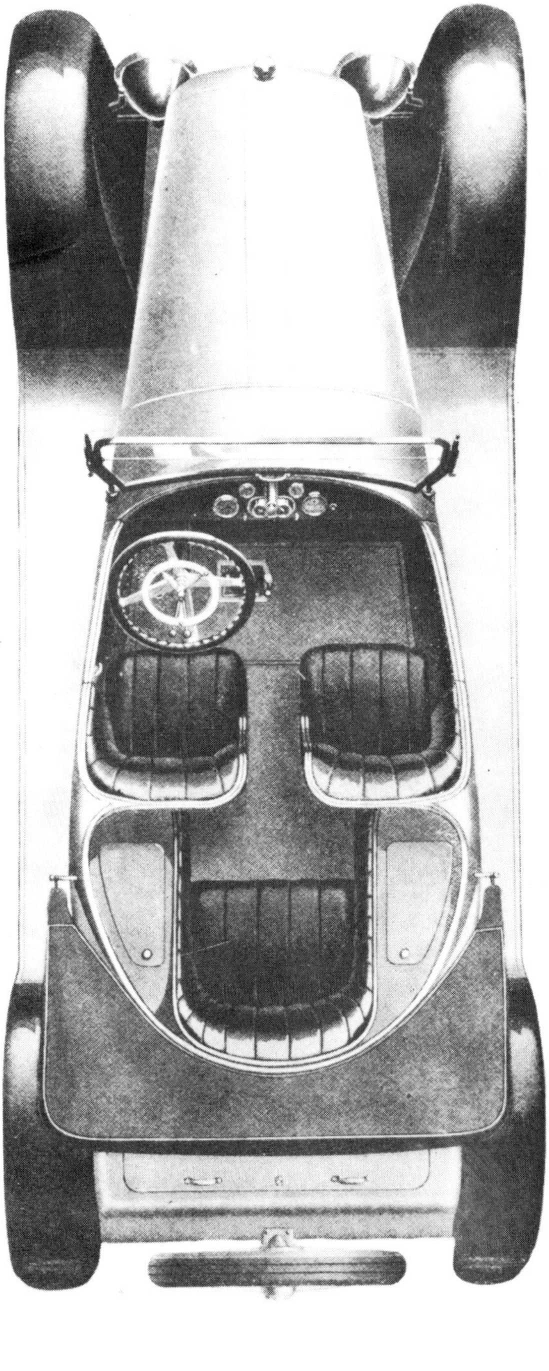

Six-cylinder Model 34 Marmon. The three-passenger roadster has unique seating arrangement.

Courtesy J. Ritter

A 1929 Franklin convertible speedster with Dietrich body, 6-cylinder engine. It was originally owned by Sir Harry Oakes.

Front view of the Franklin 147 shows the famous Chinese character-like lines typical of these models. Price, $2,885 to $7,600.

The Franklin Model 147 Pirate, body by Dietrich, has flaring doors concealing the running boards.

Courtesy Harry Moore

The engine, 490.8 c.i., was the largest displacement motor on the market at that time, by far. Its three rivals from a standpoint of sheer displacement were Cunningham with a 471 cubic-inch, Cadillac at 452.8 and Pierce-Arrow with 462 c.i. Marmon easily topped all three of these in horsepower output, its engine developing 200 at 3,400. The only engine on the road that out-powered Marmon was Duesenberg with its advertised 265 hp at 4,200, with a 420 cubic-inch straight eight.

The wheelbase of the Marmon 16 was 145 inches with 60-inch tread and 218½-inch overall length. In 1931, the year of its introduction, one completely stock sedan averaged 76.4 mph for twenty-four hours at the Indianapolis Speedway to win the Stevens Perpetual Challenge Trophy. This mark, of course, was to be eclipsed by Ab Jenkins in a lesser displacement Pierce-Arrow V-12 the following year.

The Marmon 16 close coupled sedan listed at $4,925 in 1933. Pierce-Arrow offered a 147-inch wheelbase twelve at $4,295 and Cadillac's V-12 sedan was $4,145. These and other cars that are classics today, with longer, sleeker appearances, underpriced Marmon which, too, made the mistake of trying to stay in the luxury market.

As a solution, Marmon decided on a V-12 since competitors' V-12s were outselling its Sixteen in the lower price brackets. They created a prototype V-12, which, unfortunately, never reached the market. The power plant was a V-16 cut in three pieces—the middle four cylinders eliminated and the two end sections welded together; the experimental motor developed better than 150 hp.

The V-12 reportedly could cruise effortlessly all day at 80 but it never went into production, for the Marmon Company went into receivership in 1932 and was re-formed as the Marmon-Herrington Co., truck, bus and military vehicle manufacturers. Howard Marmon continued to use his V-12 as his personal car until the time of his death in 1943.

Mention air-cooling around a group of auto enthusiasts and you will be amazed to find the number of adherents to the old waterless cars. Those who favor the antique category will talk for hours about the design of the Knox air-cooled with its corrugated brass fins surrounding each cylinder like porcupine quills. They'll also talk about the 1908 desert trials in which the six-cylinder Franklins without a drop to drink ran faultlessly for three hours in a test procession moving through New Mexico's dust and heat at a rate of 1 mph while the water-cooled entrants boiled away their coolant in less than thirty minutes.

Strongest among the air-cooled enthusiasts are those who favor the air-cooled versions of the '20s and '30s. Some of them stand by Fox, designed by Ansley H. Fox, who turned out approximately 3,500 50-hp air-cooled, six-cylinder, overhead cam and valve cars with magneto ignition at his Philadelphia Motor Car Co. The air-cooled

Franklin's last year of production, 1934, offered this supercharged V-12 LeBaron sedan.

Courtesy C. W. Wallerich

fans have their own club, the H. H. Franklin Club, with headquarters at 1405 East Kleindale Road, Tucson, Arizona, and represented among their membership are air-cooled cars of all eras. But the bulk of these fanciers favor Franklins.

Unquestionably, the pinnacle of the Franklin's career, which extended from 1902 through 1934, occurred when it introduced its V-12 in 1932. During a period when Cadillac, Packard, Marmon, Lincoln, Peerless, Auburn, Pierce-Arrow were also looking for the rainbow with Twelves and Sixteens, LeBaron styled the '32 Franklin bodies which included the extension of hood panels straight back to the windshield and door lines, giving a lengthened hood appearance and creating the illusion that there were possibly even more than twelve cylinders underneath.

Interiors of the Twelves were lushly finished with Australian wool broadcloth upholstery, velvet carpets, silk window shades, polished burled walnut window and cowl trim. The limousines had a rear compartment clock and telephone.

The wheelbase was 144 inches with a 62-inch tread. The supercharged engine with its twelve cylinders of 3½-inch bore by 4-inch stroke developed 150 hp from its 398 cubic inches. Two banks of cylinders were mounted at a 60° angle and the V-type twelve with cooling fins around each cylinder was well designed for air-cooling, since a forced draft led directly into the space within the V.

In 1932 the brougham model listed at $4,400. In 1933, in order to attract more sales, the price was reduced to $3,885 and in its last year of production the same basic model dropped to $2,885. But Franklin sales continued to lag, due largely to a public apathy toward air-cooling plus the Depression hangover which affected the entire industry.

There were other excellent Franklins; the six-cylinder Model 147 was another favorite, with body styling on these 132-inch wheelbase cars with their air-cooled 100 hp plants by Dietrich, Brunn, and other fashionable coach builders of this period.

Frank B. Stearns of Cleveland, Ohio, built his first car in 1896. In 1898, the F. B. Stearns Co. was organized and twenty cars were built and sold the following year. In 1912, the Stearns-Knight was born when the company discontinued poppet valve engines in favor of sleeve valve installations. Stearns sold his interest in the company in 1918, and in 1925 Stearns-Knight was bought by Willys Overland, who continued to manufacture silent sleeve valve jobs until 1929.

The famed Minerva was one among several European cars which used Knight-type motors in many of its models. The Willys-Knight, R. and V. Knight were two others of the many making use of the design. From a luxury standpoint, the Brewster and the Stearns-Knight were the outstanding exponents of the design. And though Brewster's decade of luxury auto

One of the country's top custom coach builders was Brewster of New York. From 1915 on, for ten years, Brewster built luxury cars powered by Brewster-Knight engines. Below is 1917 Brewster town car.

Amcng the most impressive of the Stearns-Knight eight-cylinder deluxe models of 1928 was the 145-inch wheelbase chassis with an all-weather town cabriolet body, custom-built by the famous Brunn.

Another body by Brunn on the handsome custom-built convertible coupe, above. It is a 1929 model Stearns-Knight with an eight-cylinder sleeve valved engine. Note the sun visor mounted on windshield.

Willis St. Claire stirred mechanical enthusiasm for its V-8 engine patterned after Hispano-Suiza.

Courtesy Long Island Automotive Museum

The 1919 Stutz Bearcat is considered by many an all-time classic despite its comparatively early age.

1929 model Stutz has LeBaron-designed body, is good example of fine cars turned out by this firm.

Courtesy W. A. C. Pettit, Jr.

Rakish appearance of this 1931 Stutz DV32 convertible made it a great favorite with many sportsmen.

Stutz 1932 DV32 Speedster weighs 5,100 lbs., was guaranteed to exceed 100 mph. Body by LeBaron.

Courtesy Carl H. Pennrich

One of the most beautiful of the Stutz DV32s was the aluminum-bodied Rollston 1933 cabriolet.

Jordan Speedboy of 1930 sold for $2,795. Its 85 hp, eight-cylinder engine was of L-head design.

manufacturing ended in 1925, after approximately 475 custom cars—largely ornate town cars—had been produced on its Brewster-Knight chassis, Stearns-Knights' most memorable models were to appear between 1925 and 1930.

Every automotive fan speaks fondly, sometimes even reverently, of Mercer or Stutz. Often the two are linked together because they were frequently pitted against each other in early road and track competition. Stutz received its baptism on the track when the first Stutz to be built in 1911 was helmed to eleventh finish position in the Indianapolis "500" by Gil Anderson, leading to the company's slogan, "The car that made good in a day." That same day, however, a Mercer, also first introduced in 1911, placed a car twelfth and so began a decade of rivalry.

Most memorable of the Mercers were the Type 35 Raceabouts made from 1911 to 1914; about 600 of these were produced during those four years. Though the antique car fancier scoffs at the Mercers built after the Mercer Automobile Co. folded in 1919 and The Mercer Motors Co. purchased its name and assets, the Series 6, six-cylinder overhead valve Rochester engine, which powered the 1922 through '24 models, has many adherents. The Series 6, which sold from $3,750 through $4,700, was the only production Mercer to have an engine equipped with a detachable cylinder head. The model had a consistent habit of throwing connecting rod bearings at high speed because of overly small diameter retaining bolts. This was usually corrected by knowing owners who bored, tapped and refitted the bearing caps with larger diameter bolts.

Stutz, with Mercer out of the picture, moved on to even more noteworthy models. The Indianapolis, Indiana, motor car company's finest models were its Series M, SV 16 and DV 32. Stutz during the late twenties had pioneered such features as safety glass, "side-bumper" steel running boards, double dropped frame construction for a low center of gravity, power brakes, automatic chassis lubrication, a nine main bearing crankshaft, thermostatically controlled hydraulic shock absorbers and radiator shutters.

Of all the Stutz models made between 1911 and the end of 1934 the one with the greatest sentimental appeal was the Bearcat, first introduced in the middle of the second decade, dropped from the line and back again on the list in 1931. Of the two models, one a 134½-inch wheelbase job, the other a 116-inch, the latter, known as the Super Bearcat was the most renowned and since only approximately twenty-five of these were made, few are in existence today and they are highly prized.

When you mention Jordan, the name Playboy is immediately brought to mind, since one of the most highly publicized of the Jordan products was the Playboy roadster introduced in 1929 and continued until 1930. Playboy was moderately priced at $2,695, powered by a Continental straight eight L-head of 268.6 cubic-inch displacement, developing 85 hp at 3,200 rpm. However, the lushest of the Jordan line were the Speedway series with the Ace roadster and the four-passenger Sportsman's model, both listing at $5,550. The engines were 322.25 cubic-inch displacement eights, developing 114 hp at 3.200 rpm. Jordan dropped from the automotive scene in 1930, just a year after Locomobile, whose slogan had been "The best car built

Alexis De Sahknoffsky designed the body and interior of this 1931 model Peerless custom eight.

The 1929 all-weather Locomobile cabriolet cost slightly over $5,000, had 385 c.i. power plant.

Style leader of the Jordan line in 1930 was the Speedway Model Ace; 114 hp engine; price, $5,500.

in America," was also forced from the business.

Locomobile Co. of America, Bridgeport, Conn., one of the high priced manufacturers, ranked with Pierce-Arrow, Stevens-Duryea, White, Chadwick, Crane-Simplex, Peerless and Thomas (in its earlier days) as a quality vehicle, but experienced greater popularity than all of those except Pierce-Arrow. Locomobile outlasted most of its second decade competitors and in 1927 made a stab at the more modest priced field with three 8-70 Models under $2,000. However, its late twenties Model 90, carrying price tags from $6,000 to $7,500 and its Model 48—for which prices were given only on application and ranged upward to $12,000—are today's most desirable Locomobile mementos. Of these the Sportif four-passenger model and the seven-passenger touring roadster head the list.

Ruxton made a big splash when the New Era Motors, Inc., announced its front-wheel drive car in 1928. While Ruxton may be beloved by some fanciers, largely because of its low profile, handling characteristics of its front-wheel drive and Budd bodies, other auto enthusiasts blame New Era Motors for helping push Moon, Gardner, Windsor, Kissel and several others from the motoring scene. The car, which was originally to have been called the Dolphin, was the result of a venture aimed to license other auto manufacturers to use the knuckle type front-wheel drive unit which was radically different from the Cord's geared job. Only fifty-two Ruxtons were produced and sold, their bodies worked out from stock dies owned by the Budd Manufacturing Company. Today, the Ruxton is certainly one tof the rarest, if not the most highly prized, classic.

Kissel, a Hartford, Wisconsin, producer of sports cars and commercial vehicles from 1906 through 1931 was probably at its best with its 1927 and '28 Models 65 and 75. The Model 75 on a 131-inch wheelbase would do an honest 80 mph but its crash type gearbox was a definite challenge and its quick steering made it a car that required plenty of wheel work. Of these models, the most sought and long-to-be-remembered car was the Kissel White Eagle Speedster of 1928 which with its 115 hp was claimed to be able to peak at 100 mph. This reported speed was perhaps exaggerated, but the car was a beauty in its day, quite sporting in performance.

There were many short-lived cars during the twenties, some of which weren't too bad, some quite good and some others that were real mechanical turkeys. Remember the Lone Star built in San Antonio; the Sheridan, a Muncie, Indiana, product; Beggs of Detroit; Dixie Flyer of Louisville, Kentucky, or the Halladay of Newark, Ohio. None of these five, nor the Tulsa of the Oklahoma city of that same name or Driggs of New Haven, were classics by any stretch of the imagination.

But the larger Rickenbackers, the Daniel, Phiana, Chandler, Haynes, Hupmobile, Gardner, Roamer, Windsor and Moon all had models that were more than passingly respectable in performance, appearance and appointment.

There are still true classics of the late twenties and thirties and many worthwhile vintage cars tucked away in garages and barns throughout the country. Generally speaking, the restoration of one of these to mint condition is expensive and time consuming, but it is a tremendously rewarding hobby and one that is becoming increasingly popular. •

Note the unusual headlight design on this 1930 Ruxton. The sports model shown listed at $4,600.

Courtesy J. LeRoy Forsythe

Oversize spotlight is not out of place on this 125-inch wheelbase Kissel of early 1929 vintage.

Courtesy Preston Reed

McFarlan Motor Co., produced a 1925 custom town car powered by a twin-valve six. Price, $10,000.

European Classics

Some of the greatest cars to appear on the automotive scene were turned out in the precision shops of Europe.

UNITED STATES custom body builders vied for design honors with such European coach makers as Castagna, Sala, Kellner, Henry Binder, Vanden Plas, Million-Guiet, Barker, Thrupp & Maberly, Mulliner, Franay, Figoni-Falaschi, Saoutchik, Henri Chapron, de Villars, Van Vooren, Letourneur & Marchand, Freestone & Webb, Park, Ward, Lancefield, Graber, Heinrich Glasser and Erdmann & Rossi, who were applying their talents to the finest European and even an occasional American-built chassis such as the big Duesenberg J.

British Cars

In Great Britain, many beautiful and exciting automobiles were made during the twenties and thirties. Lagonda, Invicta, SS (forerunner of the Jaguar) and the pre-1928 Vauxhalls were in this group. To only a slightly lesser degree some outstanding models of normally less-classic producers, such as Alvis with its Speed Twenty-five of 1938 and the Vanden Plas sports tourer-bodied Siddeley Special, a 4¾-liter, six-cylinder, o.h.v. twin carburetor Armstrong-Siddeley, are still coveted by lovers of fine automobiles. The Parry Thomas-designed 7-liter straight-eight Leland enhanced the name of British engineering from 1922 on when Harry Thomas drove one of his Leland production touring cars to a competition win of over 90 mph average. As recently as April 29, 1957, at the Anglo-American vintage car rally at Southampton, Long Island, a 1920 Vauxhall won the acceleration test from standing start to ¼-mile in 20 seconds.

One famous classic, Bentley, since its first model of 1921 until the present, has been built in versions ranging from 3 (183 c.i.) to 8 liters (488 c.i.). The original company, headed by W. O. Bentley, failed to weather the crash and the firm was taken over in 1931 by Rolls-Royce; the cars bearing the Bentley name were reintroduced by Bentley Motors, Limited, in 1933.

The earliest Bentley, a 3-liter, had four cylinders with four valves and two cams per cylinder. Each cam operated one set of inlet and exhaust valves. A dual magneto later replaced the original model's single mag. Dry sump lubrication was

Courtesy R. J. White

Exceptionally fine model of the original team Lagonda Le Mans four-seat tourers. The 1935 car, powered by a Meadows 4½-liter engine, won many international events.

Good example of British craftsmanship, this 4½-liter 1937 Lagonda drophead coupe has a six-cylinder 271.8 c.i. displacement engine, 129-inch wheel base; original price, $7,300.

Courtesy Basil Hooper

Courtesy Robert A. Wimbush

Sir Henry (Tim) Birkin was the principal driver of this Bentley YV 7263 which established three world's speed records. The 1927 4½-liter model (shown here in three views) saw action through 1930 when it retired from racing competition.

used with the storage tank located forward of the windshield. The original four-cylinder jobs with cylinders and cylinder head cast integrally and a low compression ratio of 4.3:1 had a top speed of better than 80 mph. The same car later lapped the higher banked Brooklands circuit at better than 95 mph.

In 1923 a privately owned 3-liter Bentley, entered at LeMans, turned in a very reliable performance. The following year a factory team, Clement and Duff, won the 24-hour event to give Great Britain its first victory in the French endurance classic and to engrave in British road and track racing annals such names as Woolf Barnato, Eddie Hall, Tim Birkin, S. C. H. Davis, Dr. J. D. Benjafield, Glen Kidston, Jack Barclay, Clive and Jack Dunfee, Clement, Duff and Oliver Bertram—all who drove Bentleys to national and international honors.

The W. O. Bentley products were destined to win the French grind four more times and in 1929 Bentleys finished one, two, three and four, an all-time record for any marque.

Today, one of the rarest of the Bentley classics is any one of the four original 4½-liter team cars, one of which is presently owned by Robert A. Wimbush of Bedford Village, N. Y. This car in 1929 averaged 89.15 mph for 2,000 miles and under Victor Bruce clocked 89.57 to win the 1929 French Montlhery event, establishing a new world's record for the course.

Three Bentleys placed second, fourth and fifth in the 1922 TT at the Isle of Man with Bentley himself driving the fourth place finisher to give the cars their earliest

Bentley 1934 Park Ward standard salon boasts a 3½-liter Rolls-Royce power plant, clean body.

impressive competition performance. As a result of this event a TT replica was produced on a 120″ chassis with a 3.92:1 rear axle ratio, which was named the Speed Model but is more commonly known today as the Bentley "Red Label," from the winged "B" radiator insignia's red enamel background. Other W. O. Bentley products are termed Green or Blue Label for like reasons.

The following year the extremely rare production "Green Labels" were built with short 96″ wheelbase and 100 mph speed potentials. These cars equipped with four-wheel brakes, twin S.U. carburetors and four-cylinder plants of 6:1 compression ratio, developed approximately 85 hp at 3,500 rpm.

The last of the 3-liter series was built in 1927. An estimated 1,625 3-liter Bentleys, at least 20% of which are still in running condition today, were produced. A 6½-liter, six-cylinder Bentley, called the "Big Six," was built in 1925 in very limited quantities and the 4½-liter jobs, sometimes called "fourpence-ha'penny," were brought out in 1927. In blown form, the Big Six made a considerable impression at closed circuit and road events throughout Europe.

The blown Bentleys are invariably referred to by members of the Bentley-Owners Club as "Blower Bentleys." Only approximately fifty of the 650-odd 4½-liter jobs were so equipped. Today, a Blower Bentley with the ribbed blower pot exposed in front of the radiator is a rare and valued version of W. O.'s handiwork.

The 8-liter models, produced just before the end of the third decade, were consid-

Enclosed 1935 Bentley Continental tourer with a 3½-liter engine has coachwork by Vanden Plas.

The 4½-liter 1937 Bentley superseded the 3½-liter models. H. J. Mulliner & Co., did body work, above.

ered the smoothest, most tractable of Bentley's passenger cars and, actually, despite the rugged man-shaking characteristics of the sports models, were as smooth functioning as any job of the era, but not as silent. Several of the 8-liters were built in sports car form. One of the huge 488 c.i. jobs with 132″ wheelbase housing its six big cylinders of 3.9″ by 5.46″ bore and stroke and 7:1 compression ratio was converted over to single-seater track form. The potent monster was clocked on the Brooklands Speedway at an average 142.6 mph for a lap record in 1928. The car later unofficially was timed at better than 143 mph. Ultimately this special was redesigned into a two-seater sports car which is still running today and plenty quick. It is thought to have a peak straightaway speed of between 135 and 140 mph—not bad for a thirty-five-year-old mechanism.

Many classic car fanciers sneer at the post-1933 Bentleys and claim that the only models worthy of the title "classic" are the W. O. Bentley products. On this basis of judgment they would be willing to concede Lagonda and Aston-Martin as classics since these cars are later representative products of W. O.'s design genius. The idea, however, that the 1933 and later Bentley is not a classic masterpiece is so much hogwash, even though the Bentleys of the Rolls area are a totally different product from their predecessors.

When Rolls-Royce took over Bentley in 1931, it completely redesigned the entire car, blending Rolls sumptuousness, silence, smoothness and durability with a fleet sports car quality. The 3½-liter result, available for the first time in 1933, was certainly a high performance car. The "Rolls" Bentley offered smoothness, quiet operation and relative fleetness with a top speed in the neighborhood of 90 mph. Silence was a new feature for the Bentley and the car was almost immediately advertised as a "Silent Sports Car."

Like Rolls-Royce and Mercedes-Benz, the Bentleys of today are certain to become the classics of tomorrow. Present day Bentleys range in price from $8,700 to $14,000 and some of W. O. Bentley's original models still bring nearly as much on the used car market as they did new, thirty or more years ago.

The advertising slogan of Rolls-Royce, Limited, lays claim quite simply to "The best car in the world." Few motorists, whatever their enthusiasm for other cars, will deny the validity of this claim. No other marque in automobiling stirs up such respect as do the products which combine the names of the Honorable Charles Stewart Rolls and Sir Frederick Henry Royce.

Henry Royce completed his first automobile in early 1904, entered it that year in the Paris Salon and won a gold medal. Royce, an electrical engineer, became at-

Brewster landau on a 1928 Rolls-Royce Phantom I chassis has separation between driver and rear seats.

Courtesy Frederick P. Thorsen

tracted to automobiling just after the turn of the new century when he bought a French-built automobile as a hobby but found it less skillfully constructed and engineered than he had expected. In a small work shop in Manchester, Royce started work on three cars simultaneously. His first completed Royce was a two-cylinder tourer of an estimated 10 hp. His other models were a three-cylinder, 15 hp, and four-cylinder 20.

Royce was fortunate at the time of the completion of his products to make the acquaintance of Charles Stewart Rolls, owner of an automobile sales agency in London, who not only had driven cars in competition on the Continent but was also an enthusiastic free balloonist and cyclist. Rolls, who had won the Thousand Miles Trial of 1900, was offered a demonstration in the four-cylinder Royce and was so impressed that he immediately agreed to handle sales. In 1906, the two separate organizations were joined to form Rolls-Royce, Limited.

The first six-cylinder Rolls-Royce was built in 1906. Shortly thereafter this Six was further refined as the immortal 40/50 Silver Ghost, which was to roll its way into classic status relatively unchanged for 19 years.

The original 48 hp, 4½″ by 4½″ bore and stroke, six-cylinder Ghost, which developed its rated horsepower at a loafing 1,700 rpm, achieved motoring immortality. The first models sold in 1907 were equipped with a 3.5:1 rear axle ratio and a four-speed gear box. The third gear was the normal high and the fourth was known as the sprinting gear. The chassis price alone for the first Silver Ghost was $4,750; Rolls-Royce did not make its own bodies until the all-steel bodied Silver Dawn model of 1949.

The Rolls Derby Plant was opened in 1908. Within a matter of a few years the R.R. was established as the quality car of all autodom. In 1911 a Silver Ghost touring car was driven non-stop from London to Edinburgh and return, then taken to Brooklands track where, without any adjustments, it was clocked at 78.26 mph. This car was strictly stock in every respect and its weight, including passengers, was 5,257 pounds. A specially designed lightweight Silver Ghost that same year clocked 101 mph on the famed British Speedway.

One 1908 Silver Ghost model, originally owned by the Hanbury Family of England, had been in regular use by that family until several years after World War II

Note complicated carburetor of R.R. engine. Plate in center allows weekly oiling of torque tube.

Courtesy George Greenberger

Springfield 1929 P.I Rolls with Buffalo wire wheels, Bausch & Lomb headlights, Brewster body.

Springfield-built 1928 Rolls-Royce convertible has gold-plated interior hardware and leather seats.

Courtesy Wendling Bros.

Courtesy S. L. Spencer

The original price of this 1933 Phantom II Rolls-Royce with Kroydon body style was about $20,000.

Courtesy Dr. W. H. Hall

Chaumont 1929 R.R. has clocked 258,000 miles up to date. Body is by Hibbard & Darrin; $19,663.

Below, beautiful Rolls Continental tourer model Silver Ghost of 1922 sold originally for $23,000.

Courtesy William G. Gregor

Park Ward did the body work on this Rolls P. II, one of the few experimental R.R.s ever released.

when the company bought it and restored it to its original condition. Today, the model will still roll out better than 70 mph with ease and has been driven more than 500,000 miles.

R.R. durability was due to the care and quality of materials specified for it by F. H. Royce. Stressed, unhardened parts of the engine and transmission were made from 3½% nickel steel as were most of the chassis bolts; all gears and transmission shafts were case hardened nickel steel; the frame was hot formed of 3½% nickel structural steel; hinges and controls were nickel silver; brake mechanisms and steering column were also cased in nickel silver; monel was extravagantly used for accessory components such as oil filters.

Contrary to a popular myth, Rolls-Royce engines are not sealed but each chassis carries a three-year guarantee on all parts other than tires, batteries, lamps, speedometers, etc., accessories not manufactured by Rolls-Royce.

After World War I, some Rolls-Royces were made in the United States. Between 1920 and 1922, the American-built R.R.'s were largely assembly jobs with chassis imported from Britain and fitted with American body work. These models, many of which are in existence today, carry the Derby chassis numbers. The American Rolls-Royces, frequently referred to by the classic fancier as the Springfield Rolls, were constructed in the Silver Ghost model from 1922 through '26. The Springfield, Massachusetts-built versions constructed between October 1922 and June '24 were right-hand drive with four forward speeds and a 12-volt system. Those constructed between October 1924 and January '25 were identical, except for a 6-volt system. From February 1925 through July '26, the Springfield Silver Ghosts had left-hand drive, three-speed transmissions and a 6-volt system. In September 1926, The Silver Ghost was finally discontinued and for two years the Springfield works built left-hand drive Phantom I Rolls-Royces with cast iron cylinder heads. From December '28 through January '31, when production of R.R.'s ceased in America, left drive P.Is of Springfield manufacture had aluminum heads.

No Rolls-Royce motor requires being run in since great pains are taken with all details in machining and assembly. The first operational check is a four-hour test during which fresh oil is pumped continually through the engine as it idles smoothly at 500 rpm. This preliminary test with its constant flow of fresh oil is designed to flush away any particles of metal or dust which escaped the eagle eyes of inspectors during the engine's construction. After the original purging, cylinder blocks are given a rough test of eight hours during which a horsepower curve is plotted. If the hp curve meets the rigid specifications, the engine is mounted in a chassis, fitted with solid tires at the rear and placed on a treadmill of steel drums. Once the engine is warmed up, the car is driven for the equivalent of 70 miles at full throttle with ever-increasing strain being placed on all gears as added drag is gradually exerted to the rapidly revolving steel drums. This typical test given to the Phantom IIs of '32 was equivalent to climbing an increasingly steep 70-mile upgrade with greater temperatures on all working parts than would be encountered in climbing the steepest

Outstanding example of fine British craftsmanship, this Daimler was specially designed and built for the King of Siam. The car is a 1923 limousine, model Double-Six. Note speaking tube above driver's seat.

mountain at the Equator. Another part of the Phantom II test of that era was to equip the chassis with a body which was specially designed to magnify any noises of overly tight, sloppily fit or out of balance parts. If the chassis passed both of these tests, it was returned for a complete engine decarbonizing and final inspection of all moving parts.

Since custom coachwork was applied to all pre-1949 Rolls-Royces, including Phantom I, II and III, no average price can be given. In certain instances, fantastic sums have been recorded. Cecily and Max OBie of New York City own a specially built Phantom I. This sedan with body by Jonckheere of Belgium, was built at a cost of $100,000 for the Duke of Windsor, in 1934. Overall length of the car is 264″; it weighs 7,200 pounds. The front seats are four-way adjustable; the ceiling is finished in red plush velvet and seats and door panels are of red and white leather while floors are fitted with heavy white pile carpeting.

Today, less than one-tenth of the company's activity is devoted to automobile production. The car division was moved to Crewe in 1945 along with its subsidiary, Bentley Motors, Limited. With the exception of the fabulous Phantom IV built expressly for Queen Elizabeth II, the Phantom III continues to stand out as the most exceptional product of a manufacturer which has been turning out nothing but classics since 1907.

Surprising though it may be, not Rolls-Royce but Daimler was the official motor car of the British Royal Family. The company's long standing connection with the Crown dates back to 1900, when King Edward VII, then Prince of Wales, ordered his first Daimler. It was Edward who at a very early date foresaw the great potentialities of the automobile and the important part it could play in the future of Britain's economy.

Largely due to Edward VII's encouragement of the industry by learning to drive a car and using one publicly at state occasions, much of the early prejudice against motor cars in England was overcome. The Royal Family's cars, with bodies by Hooper & Co., (Coachbuilders) Ltd., were designed with particularly high bodies which prevented any semblance of streamlining but did permit the King and his entourage to wear top hats, with ample clearance.

What was there about these cars that had such an appeal for royalty? Perhaps Rolls-Royce's reputation for ostentation may have led the Royal Family to accept the less conspicuous Daimler in its stead in a vague democratic gesture. More probably, it was the reputation of the Daimler for silence of operation that first appealed, for by no stretch of the imagination could the royal Daimlers be considered inexpensive automobiles. Queen Elizabeth's Phantom IV Rolls-Royce, mentioned above, was the first Royal departure from Daimler.

During Daimler's long (since 1893) career, two outstanding design features have had a particularly marked influence on the industry as a whole. Charles Y Knight of Wisconsin, had as early as 1905 worked on his design of a sleeve-valve engine since he considered that the principal weakness of the internal combustion engine was its noisy characteristic. In 1906, the Daimler Co. became interested

Victoria Eugenie, Queen of Spain, was the owner of this 1925 Daimler limousine, which has a 156-inch wheel base and was 212 inches in overall length. The automobile is in typical elegant Daimler style.

Two blocks of six cylinders, each operating on a common crankshaft with dual ignition and carburetion, were features of the 1928-1929 Daimler Double-Six (50) models. Note batteries under running board.

One of most ornate of sleeve-valve Daimler's was gold plated model designed for an Indian prince and delivered in 1930. Body, frame and springs were gold plated, hardware and instruments were solid gold.

Flexible hydraulic drive was featured in the 1931 Daimler, 436 cubic-inch 12-cylinder sports salon.

King George VI's 1937 Daimler had elaborate lamps, desk; high roof allows wearing of top hats.

in Knight's experiments and asked him to come to England to demonstrate.

The company, in order to test Knight's engines, installed them in two Daimler cars. In 1909, they ran both motors for 132 consecutive hours in bench tests, which, had the engines been installed in automobiles with standard Daimler gear ratios, would have driven them each a distance of 8,830 miles at 48.4 mph without a breakdown. Following the test, with no repairs or adjustments, the engines were installed in two other cars, driven to Brooklands and track tested for 2,000 miles.

Since the tests were conducted under the supervision of the Royal Automobile Club, previous criticism of Knight's engine as impractical and subject to breakdown was dramatically overcome. Daimler adopted the design as did the Belsize Co., of Manchester, Minerva Co., of Belgium and D.M.G. of Germany. Not until 1934 did Daimler discard the silent sleeve-valve design.

Another outstanding Daimler contribution was the flexible hydraulic drive, more commonly referred to as the fluid flywheel. Daimler Co. adopted this system of transmission in 1930, although it had been introduced many years before by Lawrence Pomeroy, the company's chief engineer, who, in 1929, became managing director. Daimler's fluid drive was the first such transmission ever to be used on a motor vehicle; it is without question the forerunner of the present day automatic transmission. Daimler installed a dashboard-mounted epicyclic pre-selector which made the entire power transmission completely revolutionary. Many automotive engineers claim that Daimler's fluid transmission and pre-selector gear box of 1930 was as important an advance as the introduction of electric ignition in place of tubular glow ignition. It freed the floorboards from the gear lever and brought armchair motoring into existence. Of course, just as the bulk of the public would praise Daimler for this engineering innovation, a minority group will forever damn them for taking the fun out of motoring, making it an old woman's activity rather than a sport.

Italian Cars

In Italy, Alfa Romeo of Milano, has enjoyed a forty-year reputation for excellence of performance and exceptional durability. Alfa reigned nearly supreme in competition circles since the introduction of its Pl six-cylinder blown job in 1923. However, though racing accomplishments were important, its spot in automobile classicdom was based on the superb sports touring models such as the 6C of 1928 through '31 and the late 8C models through 1938.

The Alfas were noted for their extremely light wheel touch and deft, precise response. In 1932, the 2.3-liter Straight Eight of 142.5 cubic-inch capacity with two blocks of four cylinders each caught the fancy of the design connoisseur. The camshaft gear train on this model was located between the two blocks since the crankshaft was divided in two sections; it rotated in ten bearings. A similar 2.9-liter version later was used in the monoposto (one-seater) racing cars that swept aside all competition until 1935, when Mercedes-Benz and Auto-Union competition teams received state support in Germany.

Less noteworthy performance-wise, but equally distinctive mechanically and more patrician in body design, was Italy's automotive pioneer and early adherent to the eight-cylinder in line design, Isotta Fraschini. Fraschini, from the time of the introduction of its first Straight Eight in late 1918 until it ceased production at outset

Alfa Romeo 1934 two-seater has eight cylinders; 225 hp at 5,400 rpm; was clocked at over 160 mph.

Alfa Romeo 8C 2.9-liter eight-cylinder cabriolet, with 1937 body by Pinin Farina, develops 180 hp.

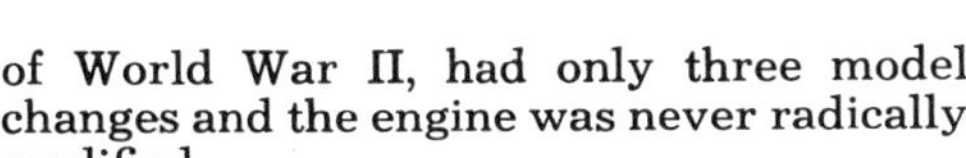

of World War II, had only three model changes and the engine was never radically modified.

Lancia was another of Italy's fine automotive products. The Lancia in its famous Lambda model, first announced in 1922, was equipped with a unique 2.121-liter four-cylinder power plant of staggered-V design. Far more exciting in performance was the larger 4-liter staggered V-8 Lancia Dilambda, which was followed progressively by an eight-cylinder Astura model, then the Augusta, Arena and Aprilia models, all V-fours. The classic enthusiast, however, is far more interested in the first three, although the tiny 1.2-liter Augusta produced amazing performance for its size. Lancia was noteworthy for originality of chassis design and the unique cylinder arrangement of its power plant.

German Cars

Mercedes-Benz was born in 1926 by a merger of the Daimler and Benz interests. The car, destined to be a thoroughbred from the start, combined companies which had truly pioneered in European automotive development.

Carl Benz had been granted a patent for a three-wheel motor car in 1884, and shortly after that had formed Benz and Company, Rhenish Gas Motor Factory, at Mannheim. Gottlieb Daimler, in 1885, introduced a four-cycle engine which included tubular glow ignition, freeing the internal combustion engine for the first time from a low-speed, 200 rpm maximum restriction placed on it by the previous sliding window type flame ignition. Daimler was the first man who had any true degree of success in harnessing an internal combustion engine to a road vehicle.

Daimler's first four-wheeler, a Victoria-type motor driven carriage, was built in 1886 and so great was the demand for his

Courtesy Hayden Shepley

An exceptionally popular automobile was the torpedo open tourer Lancia Lambda of 1925 vintage.

Courtesy Hayden Shepley

Lancia Lambda model with integral chassis and body has unusual V four-cylinder 2121 c.c. engine.

Courtesy Long Island Automotive Museum

Isotta-Fraschini was pioneer Italian motor car manufacturer. This 1914 boat-tailed speedster, Model KM, boasted 16-valve overhead camshaft four-cylinder engine, is a sports classic "par excellence."

Four-wheel vacuum servo-assisted brakes were a standard feature of 1925 50/100 Isotta-Fraschini.

Castagna used an Isotta-Fraschini 8A chassis to build this four-seater enclosed limousine body.

new high speed ignition-compression engine by such firms as France's Panhard-Levassor, that the Daimler Motoren Gesellschaft was formed in 1890. The Daimler motors (no connection with Daimler of Britain) were steeped in a tradition of speed. The two Peugeots and the Panhard which finished one, two and three in the first recorded auto race sponsored in 1894 by the Petit-Journal de Paris, over a Paris-Rouen course, were equipped with D.M.G. built engines.

In 1903 a stripped down stock Mercedes touring car, driven by Camille Jenatsky, was to defeat the finest racing cars entered by the U.S.A., Great Britain and France in the Gordon Bennett racing event, the equivalent to a world's racing championship.

Through the first two decades, Mercedes and Benz continued to gain honors. In 1911, Bob Burman in the famous Blitzen Benz created a speed mark of 141.732 mph on the Daytona sands, a mark that was to stand for eight years. In 1913, Benz won first prize and Mercedes second in the German aircraft competition. Mercedes entries scored one, two and three in the French Grand Prix of 1914, with Lautenschlager, Wagner and Salzer driving the chain drive, four-valve-per-cylinder, 4,456 c.c. displacement winners.

In 1921 the famed Mercedes 28/95, a forerunner of the Mercedes K of 1924 and Mercedes-Benz S of 1927, was introduced. The 28/95 was the first supercharged six to be built into a standard production model. It burst into prominence when driven to an overwhelming victory in the 1921 Targa-Florio Sicilian road race.

The 1924 Mercedes Ks were awe-inspir-

Courtesy J. O. Goodell

Type 8A 1928 Isotta-Fraschini convertible has straight-eight engine of 449.69 c.i. displacement.

Courtesy Brooks Stevens

Massive Isotta-Fraschini convertible, Model 8A, was one of most beautiful of European autos.

ing cars, with 148-inch wheelbase aluminum bodies, wire wheels, four forward speeds and a 1:1 ratio in high gear. Unlike other high speed cars of the day, the Mercedes could take tremendous abuse without constant tune-ups; at 35 mph the 140 hp power plant was ticking over at a lazy 1,000 rpm.

With the merger of the two companies in 1926, the K model was continued, but in 1927 the Mercedes-Benz was released in both the K model 27/110/160 (110 horsepower unblown, 160 hp blown) and the first S model, the 27/120/180. The S of 1927 had the windshield set approximately one half the distance between the two axles, giving the car an appearance of being 50% power plant, which is very close to what it was.

By 1928 the S had been brought to perfection. In stock form it had been clocked at 110 mph with a factory tune-up and factory driver at the wheel. Models straight off the floor with 1:2.76 gear ratio, however, were guaranteed 102 mph. The six-cylinder power plant of 3⅞-inch bore by 5⅞-inch stroke displaced 415 cubic inches, and with a supercharger at 3,000 rpm developed 180 hp. Valves were vertically suspended in the cylinder head, with overhead camshaft operated by the crankshaft through a vertical intermediate shaft and helical gears; twin carburetors were equipped with a controllable heater for the intake manifolds; the four-wheel brakes were internal servo operated.

In 1928 the SSK model was also introduced. This power plant had a displacement of 429 cubic inches and with a heavily reinforced Roots-type supercharger, developed 280 hp at 3,200 rpm from its twin-

Courtesy J. O. Goodell

Body work by Castagna, on this 1928 8A Isotta-Fraschini, greatly resembles that of Rolls-Royce's.

Prototype of Isotta-Fraschini 8C Monterosa of 1947 never went into production. Body by Touring.

Courtesy Captain John Leydon, USN

Mercedes-Benz 1927 Type S sports model. With blower, the six-cylinder 415 c.i. engine develops 180 hp.

Above, 1928 Type SS Mercedes-Benz touring car; 7.1-liter, six-cylinder engine; exceptional body.

Below, 1928 S 36/220 Mercedes. Exhaust headers emerging from hood are indicative of its 220 hp.

Courtesy H. P. Thorsen

ignition power plant. On all blown models the supercharger was engaged by flapping the accelerator pedal to the floor, then backing off as the supercharger cut in with its screaming challenge to competitors. The SSKs with the added horsepower, shorter wheelbase, could roll out about 130 mph; the same model with the frame disked out with lightening holes weighed only 2,400 pounds. Known as the Model SSKL, with Rudi Caracciola at the wheel, it had rolled out speeds in excess of 150 mph.

The S, the SS, SSK and SSKL were designed in the true classic manner with performance, ruggedness, responsiveness and durability incorporated in a simply styled mid-European type sports body with no superfluous trims, gadgetry or decorative effects required to spell out its purposeful appearance. The big Six Mercedes and the SS of the following year appealed, too, to the fine custom body builders, and those who could afford the $18,000 average cost of the Ss and SSs, frequently gilded the hardy lily by gracing it with a Heinrich Glaser or Erdmann & Roni body. Few of the S and SS models reached the United States and today they are among the most prized collectors items.

In the U. S., one of the most popular of the Mercedes-Benz's is the Model 540K. Though the lines of the bodies had been smoothed and the extremely stiff man-handling characteristics of the earlier models had been ironed out, the late '30s 5.5-liter straight eight, valve in head jobs were certainly not sloppy production built cars but precision instruments for travel or sport; nor was there any indication of lessened quality in their price tags which continued to hover around $17,000 to $19.000, dependent upon body styles.

The crankshaft of the 540K was fitted with nine main bearings. Compare this to any of the American classics of the same period. The power plant was supercharged and the transmission included a semiautomatic overdrive with four forward speeds. In overdrive, with a ratio of 2.8:1, the 540 could scamper along very close to 120 mph.

There were also the mid-thirties Model 500s which were plenty long on looks and near tops in performance against any car. The sheer brute power of the huge "Groser Mercedes," the 7.7-liter 150-200s with blown eight-cylinder power plants, made them the official cars for the Nazi elite, although, it is reported, Daimler-Benz entered into its capacity as official coach builder for the Hitler regime with more than a modicum of misgivings.

All Mercedes-Benz's of the '26 through '40 era are not by any means of classic caliber; there were some unexciting and routine small displacement utility cars which roughly compare with the American mid-price product of the same era.

Though Mercedes-Benz was by far the standout car in Germany, others such as Adler—manufactured by Adler-Werke in frontwheel drive version—were extremely interesting and exceptionally fine engineered automobiles. The Frankfurt am Main engineers were particularly interested in aerodynamic body design and produced some extremely beautiful small displacement two-seater sports models as well as the famous stream-lined Adler Trumph coupes. One of these, presently owned by Joe Gertler of Bronx, N. Y., though only 2 liters in displacement, ran 122 mph average for one hour at Nurburg-Ring and averaged 108 mph for twenty-four hours at the same location. The bodies and chassis of these models were designed by Dr. Porsche and executed by the Messerschmitt aircraft plant. The coupes were of four-passenger, two-door, all aluminum design with four-wheel independ-

Erdmann & Roni were the custom builders for this cabriolet on eight-cylinder 1931 Mercedes chassis.

Courtesy Marvin Safir

Model 540K 1939 Mercedes-Benz convertible with natural leather top has clean, sweeping lines.

Courtesy Lt. Col. Andrew L. Cox

Grand Mercedes of 1939, originally owned by von Ribbentrop; supercharged, 7.7 liter, eight cyls.

Custom-built, supercharged 5.4-liter 1939 Mercedes-Benz convertible, seats only two passengers.

Type 150 Mercedes has 1.5-liter rear engine. The 1935 sports roadster is extremely rare model.

Another unusual body treatment is evident on this 1938 Type 540 supercharged roadster Mercedes.

ent suspension, aircraft shocks, four-speed transmission front wheel drive and 12-inch brake drums, with brakes adjusted by turning hand wheels on each drum. They had a tremendous, 68-gallon, fuel capacity capable of 24-hour non-stop high speed run.

Austro Daimler, whose destinies at one time were directed by famed Ferdinand Porsche, also was a high quality automobile as was the Audi, produced by Auto Union. Another notable product of Auto Union was the Horch which in the late thirties was released in a 5-liter version powered by an eight-cylinder overhead valve engine equipped with a ten-main-bearing crankshaft. Aside from its considerably greater scaled-up size, the 5-liter Horch convertible coupe bore a close resemblance to the Audi, and well it might since Glaser designed both versions. The Horch 5-liter had a 132-inch wheelbase and was nearly 17 feet in overall length. The car was designed to compete with the Mercedes 500 and 540Ks. It sold for about $6,500.

Maybach was another German-built car of note. In six-cylinder version the Maybach developed approximately 140 hp. Spohn-designed bodies were mounted on 147-in. wheelbase chassis. A larger V-12 of 484 c.i. which reportedly could develop better than 200 hp was equipped with a vacuum operated pre-selector type gear box.

Throughout the thirties and particularly in its 1937 Model 328 version, the B.M.W. of Bayerische Motoren Werke, Munich, produced a finely engineered product whose scintillating performance was based largely on extremely lightweight frame and body construction. The engine of the Model 328 B.M.W. was so finely engineered that in only slightly modified form it has been adopted as the basis for the high performance British Frazer-Nash sports and competition cars and the high quality production sedan, coupe and sports models of Britain's Bristol Aeroplane Co., Ltd.

Belgian Cars

Belgium was best known for the Minerva, most frequently seen with Vanden Plas coachwork on either 6½-liter, six-cylinder Knight sleeve valve power plants or in later versions in straight eight Knight-engined form, the latter known as Model AL. At one stage Hibbard and Darrin were exclusive agents for Minerva in Paris, so that today some of the most sought-after sleeve valve classics are the convertibles with the famous V-shaped

The 1937 Kaiser Wagen Mercedes of 7.7-liter was the official car of the Nazi bigwigs. It featured bullet-proof glass, sirens and fender-mounted flashing red lights.

canvas between the doors. This is a Hibbard and Darring styling characteristic also seen in the 1929 Chrysler Imperial.

During the late twenties, another Belgian car holding considerable Continental prestige was the Excelsior. One 5½-liter, six-cylinder model with a four-speed gate-type gear box was capable of well over 90 mph. This was widely heralded as the Albert I model, in honor of the King of Belgium. Under the hood, the Excelsior was quite impressive. Its 5345 c.c. displacement six-cylinder block was equipped with an inclined overhead valve head operated by an overhead camshaft, with cylinders fed by three carburetors.

French Cars

In France, the three big Ds, Darracq, Delage and Delahaye boasted equivalent prestige to America's three big Ps, Packard, Pierce-Arrow and Peerless. The finest of the Darracqs, more frequently referred to as Talbot, were the 4½-liter, six-cylinder pushrod operated overhead valve jobs. In 1935, Talbot-Darracq was absorbed by the British Roots group and Lago—a French engineer associated with British Sunbeam Motors production—went to France to take over direction of the new firm called Automobiles Talbot S. A. The Lago-designed Talbots, 4½-liter 274 c.i. displacement jobs of 1938 through to the active war years were appealing both for performance and high quality custom coachwork.

Delage, which originally started business in 1906, was at its best from 1929 on when first a six-cylinder replaced the former small fours, and in 1930, when the Delage D8, a pushrod operated overhead valve straight eight was introduced. Some carefully tuned versions could roll out better than 100 mph. Delage went into bankruptcy in 1932 and its assets were purchased by Delahaye, one of the oldest of the French automotive concerns.

Delahaye, in the thirties, produced several cars worthy of classic acclaim. One was a 3½-liter, six-cylinder overhead valve high performance sports car, first introduced in 1936 and a 4½-liter V-12 introduced in 1937. A feature of the Delahaye was an electrically operated epicyclic cotal gear box.

Other fine cars of the classic tradition were made in France. Some models of the Renault definitely qualify; one of its most exciting versions was powered by an engine larger than 9 liters (556.32 cubic-inch piston displacement), six cylinders arranged in two blocks of three, side valves and a seven-bearing crankshaft. One carburetor served the tremendous power plant which was mounted on a 175-inch wheelbase chassis. The model, usually called the "45," was much sought after by carriage builders of the day and even with heavy formal coachwork, it could top 80 mph. In light open-bodied version, it would frequently reach 100. One model in 1926, with a lightweight fabric body and a three-carburetor intake manifolding, averaged 107.48 mph for 24 hours on the Montlhery track to set a new world's one-day record.

A distinctive feature of the Renaults until 1929 was their thermo-siphon cooling and the location of the radiator behind the engine. This led to the unknowing layman's thought that many of the production line versions were air-cooled, as the non-conventional radiator location was misleading. In 1929, when an 8-liter straight eight Renault model was brought out, a water pump was adopted for the first time and the radiator was brought forward of the engine. Most of the finer French carrossiers turned their hands to formal coachwork on the large Renaults until the outbreak of World War II.

Of the French automotive producers, the products most likely to be inspiring are those bearing the name Bugatti. Ettore Bugatti was born in Milan, Italy, in 1881. In 1909, after starting his car factory at Molsheim, France, the name Bugatti burst into prominence in racing circles when a tiny four-cylinder, four-forward speed chain-drive overhead engine car finished second at LeMans to the winning Fiat which outpowered and outweighed it

Courtesy Wendling Bros.

Upper left. Auto Union-Audi 3.2-liter, three-seater cabriolet, with coachwork by Glaser. Its six cylinders gave the 1937 car only about 85 mph.

Upper right. Karl Krone, famous European circus owner, originally bought this custom-built 1938 Maybach convertible. Coachwork by Spohn.

A classic of small sports cars, the 1934 Adler two-seater, left, displaced only 61 cubic inches. Note clean body lines, advanced streamlining.

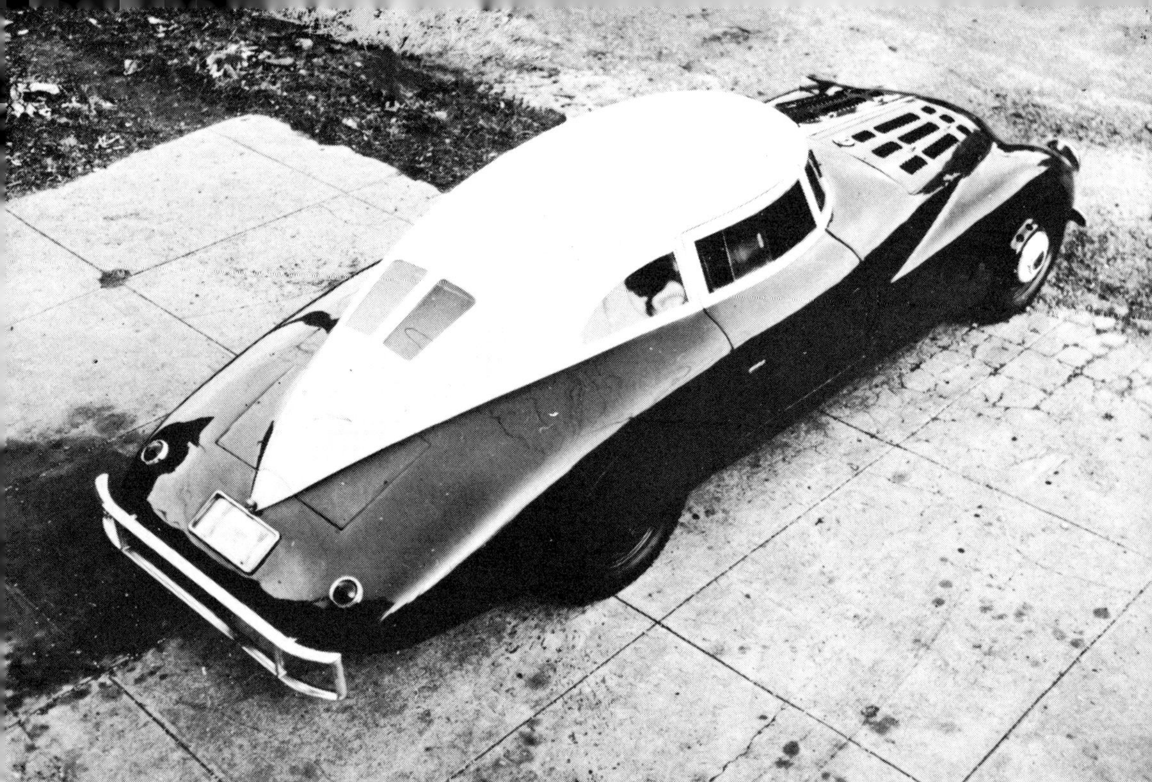

Courtesy Joe Gertler

Messerschmitt-bodied 2-liter Adler. Body designed by Dr. Porsche, car clocked 122 mph for one hour.

nearly 10 to 1. In 1921, his four-cylinder, 16-valve Brescia model—known as Type 22 and later Type 23 in slightly altered form—experienced great popularity due in part to the model's finishing one, two, three and four in the 1921 Brescia race. The Type 35, first introduced in 1924, made the real hit. This was a straight eight with 24 valves. In the original version, it had the crank shaft running in two roller and three ball bearing races with rollers also used as big end bearings. The model also was introduced as type 35C, a supercharged version, or in unsupercharged 35T form, both increased from 2 to 2.26 liters, and 35D which was a supercharged version of the 35T. The blown type 35s were capable of better than 120 mph.

Of all the Bugattis produced, the model known as the Golden Bugatti, or the Bugatti Royale, was the most exceptional. The auto, first announced in late 1928, was conceived as a car for the crowned heads of Europe. The power plant was a straight eight of 12,760 c.c. displacement. It had a nearly square bore and stroke of 125 mm by 130 mm, a block measuring 4 feet 7 inches in length, mounted in a car with a wheelbase 170 inches long and a track of 63 inches.

Tire size was 6.75x36. The crankshaft weighed approximately 200 pounds and was machined from a single billet. It was supported by nine main bearings. The engine reportedly developed 200 brake horsepower at 2,000 rpm, was equipped with three forward speeds with a 90 mph potential speed in second gear and 120 in high.

According to *Bugantics,* a publication devoted to Bugatti fanciers, the procedure of buying a Bugatti Royale was unusual, to say the least. The would-be purchaser had first to write to Le Patron, as Bugatti was called, signifying his desire to own a Royale. Le Patron would then request references of the highest description before he would consider further correspondence with the prospective client. Assuming the references were satisfactory, Bugatti would answer that he was prepared to sell the applicant a Golden Bugatti. A unique agreement was then entered into, binding to neither party: if the prospective owner did not like the car even after it had been specifically built to his requirements, he need not complete the purchase. After the initial ordering, sometimes months or more than a year would pass, then Bugatti would invite the purchaser to spend a week or so at Bugatti's Molsheim chateau. At the end of a three- or four-day stay, if Bugatti by then still approved his client, he would show him the vehicle and the owner would be initiated to the intricacies of its operation by Le Patron himself.

Clients who Bugatti deemed worthy included King Zog of Albania, King Alfonso of Spain, King Carol of Roumania, King Albert of Belgium, Andre Citroen of France. In all, only eight Golden Bugattis are thought to have been built, including one for Le Patron's own personal use.

The premium sized Bugattis, were guaranteed for the duration of the owner's life for use anywhere in the world as long as the original owner retained possession of the car. The Bugatti Royale had a chassis price of $15,000 and reportedly some of the most lavishly equipped models cost more than $40,000.

Dozens of would-be purchasers were turned down, including, according to legend, a notorious American beer baron and the wife of a Chicago meat packer.

Spanish Cars

Several interesting cars were built in Spain. One, the Nationale, was a well designed eight-cylinder 2.8 liter o.h.v. overhead cam quality car manufactured by Fabrica Nationale de Automoviles in Barcelona. Most famed of the Spanish cars, however, was the Hispano-Suiza, designed by a Swiss electrical engineer, Mark Birkigt. Pre World War I Hispano-Suizas were equipped first with L-head, then T-head engines. But during World War I, Birkigt joined forces with the French and designed for them a V-8 aviation engine which featured aluminum blocks with screw-in type steel cylinder liners. As early as 1911, Hispano-Suiza had part of its factory at Le Vallois, later Bois Colombes sur Seine in France. The balance of its production was centered in Barcelona.

Custom-built French Delahaye of 1939. Figoni and Falaschi of Paris designed and built its body.

Courtesy Henry Carpenter

Coachwork for this 1939 Delahaye six-cylinder o.h.v. was done by Henri Chapron of Paris; $14,000.

A Renault 1932 chassis was used for this custom-all-weather car by Fernandez & Darrin, Paris.

Only eight of the Bugatti Royales were made. Above, 1931 limousine of King Carol of Romania.

In 1919, Birkigt had a prototype chassis of a new six-cylinder model ready for the Paris Salon. The entire cylinder block was finished in gleaming black high luster enamel which, though being affective eye appeal wise, served the added purpose of preventing the aluminum alloy block from being affected by the deteriorating action of acids from fuel fumes and other damaging chemicals. Though the power plant was six-cylinder in line, it borrowed much from Birkigt's Hispano-Suiza aircraft engine, having the same dry steel liner cylinder construction and overhead camshaft valves. The lightweight construction scaled the entire engine to about 500 pounds. One of these models made a considerable impression in the United States when it was announced that the president of the Stutz Company had wagered $25,000 on the outcome of a 24-hour match race between a Stutz and one of Birkigt's stock cars. The Hispano-Suiza had things pretty

Courtesy Vivian Corridini

Bugatti Type 57SC, straight eight of 3.25-liter has twin overhead camshafts and supercharger.

Courtesy Vivian Corridini

Rear view of 57SC. This was the last production model ever manufactured at the Molscheim plant.

Courtesy Lt. Carl F. Montgomery, USAF

Famous Bugatti Royale has 4′ 7″ eight-cylinder block. This model reportedly cost over $47,000.

Courtesy Long Island Automotive Museum

Hispano-Suiza 1935 V-12 convertible coupe. The 9.5-liter engine offered speeds of over 100 mph.

Note elegant luggage compartment of a Boulogne model Hispáno-Suiza with 8-liter power plant.

View of famous Boulogne Hispano-Suiza engine shows the dual carburetor, six-branch manifold.

much its own way at a loping 75 mph average as the Stutz entry ran into difficulty and finally was forced to abandon the event completely.

A later model, called the Boulogne, with an 8-liter engine added further to the Hispano's prestige. About 1930, in order to cut production costs, the overhead camshaft design gave way to pushrod overhead valves, and the dry lined cylinders were abandoned for a wet cylinder type liner with rubber gasketing.

The largest of the Hispano-Suizas was a V-12 with 574.62 c.i. piston displacement which sold for approximately $18,000, with a custom built body. This was introduced in 1931. The V-12 which, though bearing the Spanish name, was built largely in France, developed 200 hp and was available in two wheelbase lengths of 135 inches or 158 inches, respectively.

Frequently a rival of Hispano-Suiza in terms of glamorous motoring in the late '20s through the '30s is Italy's Isotta-Fraschini, mentioned earlier. Typical of its leadership is the fact that it was the first car to apply brakes to front wheels and the first to have an engine with more than four cylinders in line. The company introduced four-wheel brakes to a car in 1910 and several years earlier had equipped its production models with a workable, if somewhat cumbersome, compressed air starting device. It introduced its first straight eight in 1921. This was known as the Type 8 and the motor was basically unaltered up to the outbreak of World War II, although but few Isotta-Fraschinis were produced after 1935.

In 1949, after no production of automobiles since before the war, Isotta-Fraschini was liquidated. In 1952 Fraschini was presumed to be negotiating to reform and go back into business, but to date the long promised re-entry into production has not occurred. Though the Type 8C Monterosa Isotta-Fraschini was first announced in 1947, the radically designed car which was to have a rear 90° V-8 engine never made its appearance. The Isottas, which for chassis alone once brought about $8,500 to $10,300, would not appear to be slated for production again. Italy as a producer of cars continues today with Alfa Romeo, Ferrari, Lancia and Maserati, all probable classics of tomorrow. •